The Massey Lectures Series

The Massey Lectures are co-sponsored by CBC Radio, House of Anansi Press, and Massey College in the University of Toronto. The series was created in honour of the Right Honourable Vincent Massey, former governor general of Canada, and was inaugurated in 1961 to provide a forum on radio where major contemporary thinkers could address important issues of our time.

This book comprises the 1992 Massey Lectures, "Twenty-first Century Capitalism," broadcast in November 1992 as part of CBC Radio's *Ideas* series. The executive producer of the series was Bernie Lucht.

Robert Heilbroner

World-famous economist Robert Heilbroner was born in 1919 in New York City. He studied philosophy, government, and economics at Harvard. While still a graduate student at the New School for Social Research, Heilbroner wrote *The Worldly Philosophers* in 1953. It has gone on to become one of the bestselling economics texts of all time. After earning his PH.D. Heilbroner was appointed by the New School as the Norman Thomas Professor of Economics, where he taught for the remainder of his distinguished career. Known as an unconventional thinker for integrating the disciplines of philosophy, history, and economics, Heilbroner was lauded by his peers, including celebrated economist John Kenneth Galbraith. He was granted numerous honorary degrees, won the Guggenheim Fellowship, and wrote over twenty books. He died in 2005 at the age of 85.

TWENTY-FIRST CENTURY
CAPITALISM

ROBERT
HEILBRONER

ANANSI

Published in 1992 by House of Anansi Press Ltd.

This edition published in 2006 by
House of Anansi Press Inc.
110 Spadina Avenue, Suite 801
Toronto, ON, M5V 2K4
Tel. 416-363-4343
Fax 416-363-1017
www.anansi.ca

Distributed in Canada by
HarperCollins Canada Ltd.
1995 Markham Road
Scarborough, ON, M1B 5M8
Toll free tel. 1-800-387-0117

CBC and Massey College logos used with permission

15 14 13 12 11   7 8 9 10 11

LIBRARY AND ARCHIVES CANADA CATALOGUING IN PUBLICATION DATA

Heilbroner, Robert L.
Twenty-first century capitalism

(CBC Massey lectures series; 1992)

ISBN 978-0-88784-534-5

1. Capitalism. 2. Twenty-first century — Forecasts
I. Title. II. Series

HB501.E44 1992   330.12´2   C92-095480-4

Cover design: Bill Douglas

 Canada Council
for the Arts

Conseil des Arts
du Canada

 ONTARIO ARTS COUNCIL
CONSEIL DES ARTS DE L'ONTARIO

We acknowledge for their financial support of our publishing program
the Canada Council for the Arts, the Ontario Arts Council, and the Government of Canada
through the Canada Book Fund.

Printed and bound in Canada

For Sammy,
when he gets a little older

Contents

Acknowledgements

THESE PAGES WERE WRITTEN as part of the Massey Lectures that I was privileged to give in the fall of 1992. I wish to express my appreciation for the opportunity extended to me by the Canadian Broadcasting Corporation and Massey College. I should like as well to acknowledge the extraordinarily useful and supportive criticisms of my dear friend Peter L. Bernstein and my much-esteemed colleague William Milberg.

I
CAPITALISM
FROM A DISTANCE

*History teaches nothing, but only punishes for not
learning its lessons.*
                                   — Vladimir Kliuchesky

I

CAPITALISM IS THE NAME of the economic system that dominates the world today. The central question of these pages is to ask whether we can also expect it to dominate the world during the century ahead, which sounds as if I were about to make predictions on a grandiose scale. But to the relief or disappointment of my readers, I must make clear that such is not my intention. In the 1970s I once had occasion to discuss the ability of economists to foresee large-scale events during the twenty-odd preceding years — events such as the advent of the multinational corporation, the rise of Japan as a major economic power, and the emergence of inflation as a chronic problem of all industrial nations. Not a single one of these world-shaking developments had been foretold.[1] More recently, there have been a number of equally important world-scale happenings, such as the decline in productivity suffered by all the Western powers in the early 1970s, or the striking loss of global economic leadership of the United States. How presciently were these developments anticipated by the great research institutions that carry on their continuous radar sweep of trends? The answer is that none foresaw them. Finally, there is perhaps the largest economic turning point of modern history — the collapse of the Soviet economy. I do not know of a single economic organization, including those privy to all the secrets of government intelligence services, that expected the debacle.

So I will not be so foolish as to attempt to do that which has foiled so many — namely, to predict the future of the social order in which we live. How, then, can I speak to the theme of twenty-first century capitalism? My answer is that I shall be considering the prospects for capitalism from what might be called a perspective of future-related understanding. As we will see, this is very different from the perspective of prediction. Suppose, for example, that we looked down at the spectrum of today's capitalisms from this new and as yet unexplained vantage point. We would immediately see something that would probably never enter our minds if we were interested in forecasting which countries would be leaders and which laggards in 2025. It is the remarkable fact that although Japanese, Swedes, Americans, Canadians, or for that matter, French, Germans, English, and Italians, do not have the same habits or customs, do not agree about many political means or ends, and largely lack a common sense of humour or even of civic duty, they can nonetheless carry on an extremely important, demanding, and complex task with surprising unanimity of understanding and purpose: they can do business together. That is, they can transact exchanges in the marketplace, negotiate around the bargaining table, or engage in boardroom conferences as persons who see at least one aspect of life in much the same way. That aspect concerns the manner in which economic life is organized.

Thus, looking at capitalism from this unaccustomed perspective, puts into our hands a way of peering into the future that we would not have if we approached the problem from the viewpoint of one country, even one that we know very well. The difference is that we become aware of capitalism as a system with a basic orientation discoverable in all its individual national embodiments. Only by becoming aware of this orientation can we hope to discover whether there is a logic at work behind the movement of things — a logic that enables us to think about twenty-first century capitalism in terms that will be relevant whether we are citizens of Canada, the United States, Sweden, or Japan. The predictions we all make, like the hopes and fears we all entertain, will not necessarily be any more accurate for being based on such an understanding, but they are much less likely to be wrong or misguided in the sense that they have overlooked the requirements of all capitalist systems, and therefore of any of them.

Thus an attempt to rise above capitalism should help us think about what twenty-first century economic society might become, while still remaining capitalist; and it will help us think about where our own country might lie within those boundaries of possibility. It may even assist us in stretching our imaginations to conjure up what life might be like on the other side of those boundaries, where capitalism was no longer the organizing principle of economic life.

II

BUT WE CANNOT INDULGE ourselves in such an exercise of imagination until we have performed a more immediate investigation, namely, to make ourselves more familiar with what capitalism looks like from our elevated vantage point. I propose to do so by looking at a part of the world that is unmistakably not capitalist, and then by asking a very odd question about it. I have chosen the society of the !Kung — the so-called Bush people of the Kalahari Desert in southern Africa, whom we visit at the moment when Gai, a Bushman hunter, has just brought down a gemsbok with a well-aimed arrow and is about to divide up the kill. The anthropologist Elizabeth Marshall Thomas describes the scene in her classic account of the !Kung people*:[2]

> Gai owned two hind legs and a front leg, Tsetchwe had meat from the back, Ukwane had the other front leg, his wife had one of the feet and the stomach, the young boys had lengths of intestine. Twikwe had received the head and Dasina the udder.
>
> It seems very unequal when you watch Bushmen divide the kill, yet it is their system, and in the end

---

* The ! mark denotes the "click" language of the people.

no person eats more than the other. That day Ukwane gave Gai still another piece because Gai was his relation. Gai gave meat to Dasina because she was his wife's sister. . . . No one, of course, contested Gai's large share, because he had been the hunter and by their law that much belonged to him. No one doubted that he would share his large amount with others, and they were not wrong, of course; he did.[3]

Now for the odd question I mentioned earlier: *Does one need a knowledge of economics to understand what is going on here?* Of course we need to know a great deal about the specific culture of the !Kung — their customs and beliefs, patterns of family relationship, and the like. But economics? Perhaps I can make the question less odd by turning it around. Let us suppose that a group of the !Kung somehow arranged a return journey under the guidance of an anthropologist friend who brought them to visit Toronto, Paris, New York, or wherever. Would they need a knowledge of economics to understand what they saw in these strange places?

This time the question is much easier to answer. I am sure we would agree that life in a Western city would be incomprehensible without some understanding of economics — I do not mean the stuff of textbooks, or even the ability to understand the financial pages, much less the front pages of newspapers. I mean a general comprehension of what is meant by "work" and the rights it confers to remuneration, or a familiarity with the purpose of those discs and paper rectangles called "money," or some vague idea of why the numbers of discs or paper rectangles required to take possession of the very same item may change from one day to the next. All these commonplace things would be utterly mysterious to someone who came from a primitive society. There is no "work" performed among the !Kung, although, of course, there is a great deal of toil, because work implies complex legal and social arrangements that are completely absent in a primitive culture;[4] there is no idea of money and therefore of prices. At this basic level, then, there is as little need for a knowledge of economics to understand Kalahari life as there is an indispensable need for it in Toronto or New York.

The odd question now begins to point towards our central inquiry into the nature of capitalism. Why is there no "economics" in !Kung society, whereas economics seems to pervade life in Western countries? The answer cannot be that Kalahari people do not carry on the fundamental economic activities of a modern society, albeit at a much simpler technological level. Primitive societies perform the tasks necessary for their maintenance and continuance exactly as do the most advanced societies — the !Kung sustain their bodies, replenish their households, repair or build their shelters, make tools and implements, embark on long and arduous journeys. If we say that there is no obvious economics in the Kalahari, we cannot mean that advanced societies perform essential undertakings that are absent in their distant precursors.

To understand why we sometimes do and sometimes do not need to know economics to understand society we must embark on one more journey of the imagination. This time we do so by turning the pages of an immense historical atlas that describes the thousands of recognizably different societies in human history, all of which, of necessity, have coped with the problems of producing and distributing the wherewithal for their continuance. In this atlas the societies in which we will recognize the telltale characteristics of capitalism are but a tiny handful, grouped in the last pages of the book, where — I do not have to say — they have expanded their influence virtually around the world, presenting us finally with the opportunity to discover the unique properties of capitalism for which we are searching.

III

TURNING THE PAGES of this historical atlas is interesting for two reasons. First, we are struck by the extraordinary variety of ways in which human communities have wrestled with what we might call the Economic Problem. No two societies seem to have used exactly the same ways of mobilizing and marshalling their work forces or of distributing their product. There are many ways to raise crops, spin thread, build houses, wage war. Equally great differences are visible in the means of selecting those who will go into the fields to hunt and gather, and those who will not — gender, family, race, punishment, ambition. Tremendous variations have marked the portions distributed to different members, and classes of members, of society, and equally great differences can be found in the explanation of these differences between the favoured and the unfavoured.

The second interesting aspect of the atlas of societies is the opposite of the first. It is not the variety, but the astonishing paucity of overall solutions to the problem of assuring society's material continuance. For all its variety the atlas itself is organized into only three major sections. We have already seen the first of the three divisions in the Kalahari Bush people. How do the !Kung — and, by extension, the overwhelming majority of all human societies of which we have any historical knowledge — solve the problem of producing their needed food and other requirements, and how do they distribute what they have produced in such fashion that this social effort can continue?

Direct observation quickly yields the answer. From their infancy !Kung children are taught the skills they will need and the roles they will fulfill as they accompany their elders on journeys of gathering or hunting. The essential task of training a labour force therefore takes place as part of a process of socialization, a process to which all humans must submit if they are to become acceptable members of the community. In primitive societies like the !Kung the ruling principle of socialization is obedience to age-old ways, which is why we speak of such an organization of production and distribution as an economy under the guidance of tradition.

There is a point worth making with respect to this most ancient, durable, and perhaps ultimately life-preserving of all ways of overseeing the economic problem. It is that there is no need for "economics" in studying its mode of operation. That is, there is nothing in the socialization process that calls for the special expertise of an economist. To understand the workings of Kalahari society we need an intimate knowledge of their culture, without which the division of Gai's kill would be incomprehensible; we need knowledge about how "political" decisions are made with respect to such matters as when the community will leave one campground for another; and we need some acquaintance with their techniques of hunting and gathering if we are to understand why the community goes about these particular functions the way it does.

None of the above, however, would ordinarily be called economic knowledge. Is there, perhaps, a deeper level of penetration that would give us insight into an economic motivation beneath the "surface" of society? A contemporary Western economist might suggest that such a motive can be found in the maximizing of "utilities" — satisfactions — that can be presupposed as the decisive principle behind all activities. But even if that were the case, which many besides myself doubt, it would not throw any additional light on !Kung life. Perhaps a "maximizing" impulse drives Gai to hunt and Dasina to gather, but an economist who sought to explain behaviour by utility maximizing would also have to assert that Gai's brother, who stayed behind to loaf, was also maximizing his utilities. An "explanation" that covers every conceivable sort of behaviour cannot serve the purpose of telling us what is special about one sort of behaviour.

Such an assertion does not mean there is no "economics" in the organization of primitive social life. The point, rather, is that whatever motives and pressures and shaping forces affect production and distribution, they are inextricably intermixed with the cultural or political or technological attributes of those societies. To put it differently, if we knew everything that was to be known about !Kung culture, political relationships, and technology, what would be left for an economist to find out?

In contrast to tradition the second great coordinative mechanism is called command. As the name indicates, it solves the problems of production and distribution by orders from above. These may be the commands of a pharaoh or the laws of a state; on a smaller scale they may be the authority of a headman or a community council, the orders of a plantation boss or a factory manager. Command differs from tradition in two very important ways. First, it requires an enforcement mechanism different from the internalized pressures of socialization. That mechanism is coercion — the actual or threatened use of punishment. Command backed only by the pressures of existing mores and beliefs would be no more than a form of tradition. The orders of the Roman emperors or the Soviet commissars depended on more than the internalized pressures of tradition for their obedient response — indeed, they often demanded of people that they go against the routines of the past.

And what of the economics of command? Is there such an economics in the sense of a special kind of knowledge necessary to understand the workings of ancient Egypt or the deceased Soviet Union? Of course, taking the last case, we need an understanding of the command structure itself, in this instance the Soviet planning setup. In addition we need to be familiar with problems of running large-scale organizations, such as steel plants; and beyond that, a kind of knowledge not previously needed — knowledge of the problem of meshing many kinds of outputs if the blueprint of the central planners is to be met. The collapse of the Soviet Union has alerted us to the extraordinary difficulties of acquiring this knowledge, but the knowledge itself is little more than the extension, on a giant scale, of that possessed by every factory manager. Such knowledge is very important, but I think we are more likely to call it "management" than "economics."

Thus we reach the same surprising conclusion in the case of command societies as in those coordinated by tradition. The manner by which the activities of production and distribution are coordinated in both types of economic system is so enmeshed in the culture, technology, and politics of those kinds of societies that no special domain of knowledge remains to be filled in. Once again to make the point, although there are assuredly economic problems in tradition- and command-run societies, there is no economics in either of them, no understanding that we would lack if we fully grasped their cultures, their technical means, and their political arrangements.

IV

AND SO WE REACH the market. I shall leave aside for a moment the relation between the market as a means of organizing production and distribution, and capitalism as the larger social order in which the market plays a crucial role. While we are still trying to find out where economics fits into the larger picture, let us simply look at the workings of the market through the same uncomprehending eyes as we looked at Gai distributing the parts of his gemsbok.

This time, however, let us suppose that the !Kung people, having been deeply impressed by their trip to the West, wish to create such a society for themselves. "Tell us," they ask, "is there some way we should organize ourselves to duplicate the remarkable things we have seen abroad?"

"Indeed, there is," we reply. "You must create a market economy."

"Very well," their elders agree. "What shall we instruct our people to do?"

"Aha," we answer. "The first point is that you don't tell them what to do. They do what they please. In fact, the key difference between a market economy and the economic life of a traditional community such as your own, or a command society, like that of the ancient Dahomey kingdom, is that each person in a market system will do exactly as he or she pleases."

There is considerable consternation. "You mean," a brave elder ventures, "that we do not tell our women to gather fruit or our men to hunt? That we make no provision for the building and repair of our shelters? What happens, then, if no one goes gathering or hunting or repairs our places of rest?"

"Never fear," we reply. "All these tasks will get

done. They will get done because it will be in your sisters' interests to gather and in your brothers' interests to hunt, and in the interests of others among you to repair your shelters or to make new bows and arrows."

There are expressions of unease. "But look," another says. "Suppose we risk this astonishing change. How do we know that our gatherers will bring back the right amount of food? If it is in their interest to gather food, will they not bring back more than we need, with the result that it will spoil?"

"You don't have to worry about that," we answer. "The market system will take care of the problem. If too much food is collected, no one will want it, so that its price will fall, and because it falls, it will no longer be in your sisters' interest to collect more than you need."

"Then how do we know that *enough* food will be collected?" our interrogator asks triumphantly.

"Do not fret. The market will see to that, too!"

"But what is this market that will do these wonderful things? Who runs it, for example?"

"Well, there isn't any such *thing* as a market," we explain. "It's just the way people behave. No one runs it."

"But we thought the people behaved as they wished!"

"So they do. But you need not concern yourselves. They will want to behave the way you want them to."

"I fear," the headman of the community says with great dignity, "that you are wasting our time. We thought you had in mind a serious proposal. What you suggest is inconceivable."[5]

V

OUR DEPICTION OF WHAT a market society might seem like to someone who was not exactly sure what a "price" was enables us to take the last step on our roundabout journey to forming a picture of capitalism. For we now see something that is both very simple and yet full of significance for understanding our own social order. It is that the three organizing principles of tradition, command, and market impart totally different dynamics into the societies over which they hold sway.

The dynamism of the first organizing principle is very simple. It is the rule of stasis, of changelessness, which, however, does not mean a passive surrender to fate. Many tradition-ruled societies go on long forced marches in periods of famine and drought, and in Neolithic times we know that such communities managed the extraordinary adaptation to the demands of the Ice Age.[6] Neither does the ruling importance of tradition impose an abject level of poverty, as we long used to believe. Anthropologist Marshall Sahlins has even gone so far as to call these societies "the first affluent societies," in that their established ways amply fill the expectations of their people.[7] Nonetheless, a society whose historical journey is entrusted to the guiding hand of tradition sleepwalks through history. It may make remarkable adaptations — if it did not, human society would never have survived its danger-beset infancy — but these departures from life's well-trod course are driven by need rather than adventure or a pioneering imagination.

Things are quite different when we come to societies in which command plays a central role in the production and allocation of their provisioning efforts. We do not know precisely when command began to displace tradition as a central organizing factor — the German historian Alexander Rustow has suggested that it might have begun with the Neolithic descent of nomadic horsemen onto sedentary cultivators, bringing "a new breed of man, marked by a powerful superiority . . . over two meters in height and . . . several times faster than a pedestrian."[8] In short, Rustow suggests the prototype of the centaur. All that we know from the historical record, however, is that in parts of the world as far separated as Egypt and Central and South America, societies appeared whose social structures resembled the phenomenal pyramids they built. Undoubtedly, such formal social hierarchies were preceded in many parts of the globe by less formally stratified kinship societies.[9]

What is important for our purposes is that in all these societies command played a crucial role in their provisioning arrangements, which is not to say that tradition ceased to exert its steadying influence. Writing of ancient Egypt, Adam Smith notes that each person was supposed to follow the trade of his father, and was supposed to have committed some "hideous sacrilege" if he did not.[10] But the rut of tradition could never have guided the Egyptians or the Incas or Mayans into the construction of their extraordinary monuments, temples, and palaces. Neither could tradition have provided the goods and services that sustained the armies of Alexander or Caesar, not to mention the huge military provisioning of both sides in World War II.

Command therefore interests us because it is par excellence the mode of organization required to effectuate deliberate changes in the trajectory of society. War, revolution, or any major societal undertaking — the provision of a welfare system, for instance — may utilize many of the dependable behavioural traits of tradition and the much more flexible means of the market, of which I shall speak next. But command is the indispensable means of purposefully changing the ways and means of production and distribution, whether change itself originates in an imperial decree or by democratic vote.

So, finally, we come to the market, the organizing principle of capitalism. A capitalist order also depends to no small degree on the steadying influence of tradition — could we run a market system without the socialized trait of honesty? — as well as on elements of command; behind the contracts we sign are the courts that will enforce them. But it is clear that the impetus given to a market-organized system is very different from that of tradition or command. If traditional society sleepwalks through history, and command society pursues the goals of powerful individuals or institutions, market society is in the grip of subterranean forces that have a life of their own.

The principle of motion imparted by these forces

gives us a special kind of dynamism to which we can finally bestow the title of "economics." We are all familiar with this dynamism, whether or not we have ever read a book on the subject of economics. In its most dramatic form the dynamism has taken the form of waves of invention that have altered not only the productive capabilities of society but its social composition, even its relationship to nature itself. The first of these was the Industrial Revolution of the late eighteenth and early nineteenth centuries that brought the cotton mill and the steam engine, along with the mill town and mass child labour; a second revolution brought the railway, the steamship, and the mass production of steel, and along with them a new form of economic instability — business cycles; a third revolution introduced the electrification of life and the beginnings of a society of mass semiluxury consumption; a fourth introduced the automobile that changed everything from sex habits to the locations of centres of population; a fifth has electronified life in our own time. The foregoing list, of course, is arbitrary. What was arresting about the dynamism was that change itself became the norm of daily life. Over the entire previous history of humanity children had lived material lives that were essentially the same as those of their parents, accidents of war or natural disaster always excepted. From the mid-nineteenth century on that sense of continuity was ever more noticeably displaced by a sense of immanent change.

The continuous remaking of the social environment is assuredly the most noticeable aspect of the market's impact on social provisioning, but it is not the most significant. The deeper aspect of this kaleidoscopic changefulness is that it conceals a kind of orderliness, whereby the forces that are unleashed work blindly but not haphazardly. Quite to the contrary, there are control mechanisms, feedbacks, and self-generated limitations built into the torrent of market-driven change, so that as we look back on the historic trends and patterns of production and distribution, we can see that the working of the capitalist economy gives evidences of systemic patterns, of a kind of grand historic trajectory, a certain orderliness.

What are these patterns, this orderliness, this trajectory? What are the sources of the energy, the relentless, ubiquitous pressure for change that has been capitalism's contribution to history, for worse as well as better? These questions are matters for subsequent chapters. I must end this one on the theme with which it began — the predictability of our futures. As I said earlier, the future of the particular capitalism in which we live is marked by a very high degree of unpredictability, due to the fact that so much of its inner tendency to change can be encouraged or blocked, used or abused by the political processes that are inextricably a part of every capitalist nation. I can therefore imagine successful capitalisms and unsuccessful ones over the coming decades. Indeed, if I had to make a single prediction concerning the outlook for twenty-first century capitalism, that would be it.

But we have now seen that capitalism is unique in generating persistent and powerful tendencies to change. Here is the property that enables us to speak about its future in an *analytical* way that we cannot apply to any other social order. I do not want to anticipate ensuing chapters by speaking now about what this analytic property might be. Suffice it to say that it forms the basis of the marvellous scenarios by which the great economists from Adam Smith through John Maynard Keynes described capitalism's future path. As in the case of Marx, Smith's and Keynes's predictions of capitalism's future were not fully realized as a whole, although again like Marx's, remarkably farsighted in many respects. As I have said, I will not be so foolish as to attempt what these great masters of economic analysis have failed to achieve — that is, to lay out a scenario that will anticipate with disconcerting accuracy the changes of capitalism as an overarching social order. Their efforts will help us to see what it is about this system that enables us to think about it in such a remarkable way. Capitalism carries us all along into futures that are unforeseeable, and yet the manner in which those futures will be formed and shaped is far from being utterly unpredictable.

II

THE DRIVE
FOR CAPITAL

I

CAPITALISM, I HOPE we now see, is a more remarkable system than it appears to us, who live inside it as fish live in water. The preceding chapter was primarily devoted to making us sense the profound differences between this system and other societies dominated by tradition and command. Now it is time to turn our attention exclusively to the question of what capitalism is rather than what it is not.

Certainly capitalism's most striking historical characteristic is its extraordinary propensity for self-generated change. If capitalism is anything, it is a social order in constant change — and beyond that, change that seems to have a direction, an underlying principle of motion, a logic. Tracing the differences between the Western world of the 1700s, 1800s, 1900s, and today, we all feel a kind of developmental thrust at work — a thrust that enables us to talk about its history in different terms than those we might use in speaking of the history of the great Asian kingdoms or the Roman Empire. In large measure the purpose of this book is to discover the extent to which we can, in fact, construct a coherent and comprehensible past from which we can extrapolate a future based on more than just hopes and fears.

That larger purpose obviously hinges on an understanding of the energy that capitalism generates as a battery generates electricity. Everyone knows the source of this unique social voltage. It is the activity that lies at the heart of the order — the drive to get ahead, to make money, to accumulate capital. We will use the last phrase because, as we will see, there is an integral connection between "capital" and the system that is built on its name — a connection that is veiled, or even concealed, in the everyday terms of "getting ahead" or "making money." Our first order of business is accordingly very clear. It is to look into what we mean by the word that has become not just the name, but the identifying badge of the social order in which we live.

Surprisingly, capital is not the same thing as wealth. Wealth is a very ancient aspect of human civilization, but the drive to amass it, which we can trace back to the Egyptian pharaohs, has never become a force for continuous and deep change. Egypt was much the same when Napoleon conquered it in the early nineteenth century as it had been three thousand years earlier. In similar fashion the Incas and Mayans, or the rulers of India or China, accumulated vast treasuries of gold and built magnificent palaces and temples, but there was never anything in their long histories that even vaguely resembled the developmental logic we feel in the past three hundred years of Western history. I have already stated the reason: wealth is not capital.

What is wealth? We can approach the question by

looking at something even older than gold hoards and majestic buildings. I have mentioned that primitive societies may have enjoyed the affluence of contentment, save when nature went against them. Let me now add that many such societies also created monuments that required lengthy and arduous labours: I think of Stonehenge or the famous carved heads of Easter Island, the Lascaux cave paintings, or the great totem poles of the North American coast. Was this wealth? I think not. I would call such creations objects of virtue. As such, they were embodiments of the community's spiritual life — testimonies to its observance of time-honoured ways, placatory offerings to an animate nature.

Wealth is not an object of virtue. It is a symbol of power and prestige, usually accruing to the personage to whom it belongs, and to a lesser extent to the society in which it is found. The very word *belongs* tells us something about wealth that differentiates it from objects of virtue. It is that wealth is inextricably associated with inequality. We get this insight from a most unlikely source, the first of the great philosophers of capitalism, who wrote: "[W]herever there is great property, there is great inequality. . . . [T]he affluence of the rich supposes the indigence of the many." It is Adam Smith speaking, not Karl Marx.[11]

The matter of inequality deserves some attention. Smith was aware that the desire for riches needed some explanation, and he found it in two benefits that wealth bestowed. The first was esteem, which is based on unequal status. "The rich man glories in his riches," Smith writes, "because he feels they naturally draw upon him the attention of the world.

At the thought of this, his heart seems to swell and dilate itself within him, and he is fonder of his wealth on this account, than for all the other advantages it procures him."[12] The second reason was rooted in another source of the difference that wealth introduced. "Wealth," Smith writes, quoting Hobbes, "is power." Smith quickly goes on to say that the power conferred by wealth is not political or military, although it may be a stepping stone to the latter. It is "the power of purchasing; a certain command over all the labour, or over all the produce of labour which is then in the market."[13]

The element of inequality here is revealed in the term *command*. Smith does not mean that wealth simply allows two equally circumstanced individuals to exchange their services on a mutually satisfying basis, using money as a convenient way of simplifying the transaction. He means that a lack of wealth may force a less favourably circumstanced individual to enter into a market relation with a more favourably situated one, purely because of the difference in their situations. It hardly comes as a surprise that the rich are in a position to enjoy a disproportionately large share of society's goods and services. What may come as an unaccustomed thought is that the very concept of wealth implies such an inequality, and that a society of equals-in-wealth, although it enjoyed the pleasures of the *Arabian Nights*, would of necessity be a society in which there was no economic power.

At this juncture we arrive at an aspect of ownership that has special importance for capitalism. It is the inequality between the owners of the means of production and those who work with these means — that is, between capitalists and "their" workers. Looking back for a moment at Kalahari society, we can doubtless find a degree of inequality among the personal effects or weapons that are owned by various members of the community. But the idea that a rich Bushman might own all the tribe's weapons, so that Gai would have to rent his bow and arrow to feed his family, or that he might even have to become an "employee" of the rich Bushman in order to feed himself, would be as unthinkable in Kalahari culture as it would be to us if anyone in our society could walk into a factory and make free use of the equipment that was there. This right to deny access to the means of production is assuredly the central advantage conferred by wealth in capitalism. An individual who owns no capital is perfectly free to labour as he or she wishes, and may, in fact, become very successful using only the property of his or her body — actors or singers, as cases in point. But anyone who has no such personal talents must pay for the privilege of making use of wealth that belongs to another. This reality puts into a different light the institution of "wage labour," which is the manner in which the labour of individuals is marshalled and remunerated under capitalism.

II

Is CAPITAL WEALTH? Yes and no. Capital is certainly wealth, insofar as one who possesses capital is usually a person who enjoys esteem and who wields power in the marketplace. The question, then, is whether wealth is capital, and the disconcerting answer is that sometimes it is and sometimes it is not.

The difference lies in the peculiar nature of capital. Capital is wealth whose value does not inhere in its physical characteristics, but in its use to create a larger amount of capital. Typically, this use takes place as money is converted into commodities such as raw materials, the raw materials converted into finished goods and services, and the finished goods sold on the market — not to make a profit and retire to a life of ease, but to buy more raw materials to start the process over again. As a consequence of this endless turnover, the physical characteristics of commodities have nothing to do with their function as a means to wealth: a capitalist can get rich on coal or scrap metal, which no one could imagine as wealth. By the same token, a Rembrandt painting, which is certainly an embodiment of wealth, does not become capital unless it is no longer wanted for itself, but as a stepping stone for amassing still more capital. Then the possessor of the Rembrandt becomes an art dealer. Capital thus differs from wealth in its intrinsically dynamic character, continually changing its form from commodity into money and then back again in an endless metamorphosis that already makes clear its integral connection with the changeful nature of capitalism itself.

What drives this process that Marx called the self-expansion of capital? At this focal point of our analysis our understanding becomes uncertain. Economists speak of the never-ending expansion process as reflecting the drive to "maximize utilities," a view of which I spoke sceptically in the previous chapter. The vague motive of "maximizing" our satisfactions seems inadequate to account for the insatiability of the drive that Marx described as "Accumulate! Accumulate! That is Moses and the prophets."[14] Somewhere between the two is Adam Smith's assertion that we are the creatures of a "desire of bettering our condition" — a desire that he said "comes with us from the womb, and never leaves us till we go into the grave" — and his further description of the object of this desire as an "augmentation of fortune," which is to say, making money.[15]

I think myself that the unappeasable appetite for expanding capital is better understood as a manifestation of those drives that in earlier societies took the form of illimitable expansions of empire or a godlike glorification of kings. The empty maximizing of utilities and the rather mild "bettering our condition" by making money, then take on their necessary urgency by linking the drive to amass wealth with unconscious motives, probably derived from infantile fantasies of omnipotence. In a moment I shall suggest why, in our society, these fantasies take the form of an expansion of capital.

But there is a second motive that supplements and perhaps exacerbates the first. It is that the consequence of each capitalist seeking to expand his scope of operations soon leads to the collision of capitalist against capitalist that we call competition. "One capitalist always kills many," Marx said.[16] Thus there is an element of the spirit of war — partly aggressive, partly defensive — added to that of sheer aggrandizement. From this viewpoint capitalism appears not merely as a society characterized by constant change, but as one in which the pursuit of capital fulfills some of the same unconscious purposes as did military glory and personal majesty in an earlier time.

III

THESE REFLECTIONS SHED some light on an aspect of capitalism that is often made the subject of pious lamentations, but they do not explain why the rage for accumulation did not appear much earlier in societies under the management of tradition or command. Insofar as we often hear that the profit motive is an expression of human nature, one would think we could find the accumulation of capital far back in the past. Yet we hear little about it before capitalism appears on the scene in the eighteenth century.

We have already seen the reason. Wealth is not the same thing as capital. Julius Caesar was given the governorship of Spain with its great mines from which he returned in a few years a wealthy man. But the accumulation of capital as a driving, transforming social process required more than the enrichment of successful generals. For one thing, economic life had to be raised from the low regard in which it was held — "devoid of nobility, and hostile to perfection of character," in the words of Aristotle — to something approaching respectability. As part of this process, a semi-independent "economy" had to be wrenched free of the enveloping state. And underlying the whole, a web of transactions had to be enlarged until it reached into the very life processes of society itself. Until the most fundamental activities of production were brought within the circuit of transforming money into commodities and commodities back into more money, a capitalist social order could not take root. Only then could the accumulation of capital inherit the fantasies of power that earlier fastened on exploits of glory and adventure, with the difference that the drive for capital would be open to a far larger number of the population than the chance for military or political distinction — in theory, open to all.

What brought about so all-pervasive a change? The precipitating event was the fall of the Roman Empire itself, a catastrophic "event" that stretched out over some four hundred years. The fall of Rome was crucial not only because the social order of the Empire was at every level incompatible with a capitalist order, but because its shattered ruins provided an extraordinary setting in which such an order would emerge — slowly, painfully, and without any sense of fulfilling a historic mission during the thousand-year period we call feudalism. The often noted failure of capitalism to appear spontaneously more than once in world history is likely due to the fact that this social setting has never appeared elsewhere.

We can only trace the barest narrative of that thousand-year birthing process. The disappearance of the Empire left Europe without unifying law, currency, and government, broken into a crazy quilt of isolated and self-dependent towns, manorial estates, and petty fiefdoms — a catastrophe like that of the collapse of the Soviet Union, magnified a hundredfold. It was, however, the very fragmentation of feudal life that paved the way for the transformation that followed. By the ninth century — four hundred years after the "fall" began — pack trains of merchants were beating their way from one manor to the next, accompanied by armed retinues to fend off attacks by robber barons. Gradually, these merchant adventurers insinuated themselves into the affairs of the manor and especially the town so that by the fourteenth century — we are now almost a thousand years into medieval history — their burgher descendants had become the political authorities of expanding "burgh" or urban life. Here they played a role that was both indispensable for the evolving feudal order and ultimately subversive of it — essential because the feudal rulers were continually forced to turn for loans to their resident burghers, some of whom were by now very rich; subversive because the commercial way of life for which the lenders stood was ultimately incompatible with feudal dominance. By the end of the seventeenth century a bourgeois (burgher) class was already a political power in England; by the end of the eighteenth century it was the real master of France; by the end of the nineteenth century, the dominant political force in the world.

With the coming to power of the bourgeoisie there arose, as well, the lineaments of a new social order in which new money-minded values were perhaps the most noticeable aspect, but the spread of a new form of economic life was by far the most important. In the country the institution of serfdom, in which the serf paid a portion of his crop to his lord and kept the rest for himself, gave way to a quite different institution in which a capitalist farmer paid his hands a wage, but owned the whole of the product they brought forth. In the town the relationship of master and apprentice, under the strict supervision of guild rules, became that of employer and worker, under no regulation save the marketplace for labour. In the big cities money-making moved from the suspect periphery of life to its esteemed centre.

Thus the institutions of feudalism disappeared, not without bloodshed, and in their place appeared those of an order that Adam Smith called the Society of Perfect Liberty. The name referred to economic, not political freedom, and by our standards was very far from perfect — for nearly a century union organizers could be "transported" to Australia. Nonetheless, under a Society of Perfect Liberty workers could move freely from one location or occupation to another, which as serfs and apprentices they could not. Incidentally, the word *capitalism* did not yet exist in Smith's time, and Marx himself never used it other than in correspondence. As the term denoting the water in which we swim, *capitalism* entered the English language sometime in the latter part of the nineteenth century, perhaps in Arnold Toynbee's great work on the Industrial Revolution. It has been with us ever since, although its checkered past and problematic future incline some to prefer "free private enterprise system" with its more upbeat connotation.

IV

THE EMPLACEMENT OF CAPITAL ACCUMULATION as the moving force of the new social order makes clear why capitalism revolutionizes material and social life in a manner that imperial kingdoms, for all their pyramids, hoards of gold, or fantastic palaces, did not. The reason is that the drive for capital is directed at the foundation of society, not at its apex. The continuous conversion of commodities into money is most readily achieved across the broad spectrum of production, where it acts as a powerful force to augment the quantity and change the quality of output. The amassing of wealth in the form of monuments and treasuries has no such effect.

Adam Smith made this expansion of production a central feature of a Society of Perfect Liberty. Expansion begins, as Smith explains, because the most readily available means for a capitalist to better his condition is to save a portion of his profits and invest it in additional equipment, thereby adding to the potential output of his enterprise, and thus to his future income. In the famous opening pages of *The Wealth of Nations* Smith describes how the process works in a small pin "manufactory," employing only ten men. By dividing the manufacturing process into separate steps, each performed by a separate person, often aided by machinery, the ten workers were able to make more than forty-eight thousand pins in a day. "[I]f they had all wrought separately and independently," Smith observes, " . . . they certainly could not each of them have made twenty, perhaps not one pin in a day."[17]

The accumulation process thus exerts its immediate impact on the social environment by multiplying the productivity of labour. Smith explains the increase by the encouragement of the workman's "dexterity," the saving of time previously lost in "sauntering" from one task to another, and the more ready mechanization of "divided" labour. Nowadays economists emphasize the more innovative aspects of technology as the source of growth — not so much the division of labour, but the introduction of new products or new processes. In Smith's vision we imagine a society in which output increases, but the product remains the same. It is characteristic of Smith's lack of interest in institutional or organizational change that he expressed little confidence in the managerial capabilities of the "joint-stock" enterprises that were beginning to appear.[18]

In the vision that has largely displaced it — one associated with the work of Joseph Schumpeter in the 1930s — Smith's manufacturer soon finds the market for pins glutted but discovers another means of expanding his capital by varying his product, perhaps producing pins with coloured heads. Thereafter his son takes a chance on a new invention called "safety" pins, his grandson moves into paper clips, and their descendants take the leap into zippers and Velcro. My illustration draws on the Victorian image of family capitalism, but Schumpeter's insight was that the most formidable means of capital accumulation was the displacement of one process or product by another at the hands of giant enterprise. He called the process "creative destruction," and it remains the central agency of change in all advanced capitalist economies.

Whether carried out by Smith's pin factory or Schumpeter's innovating corporation, accumulation changes the larger society in two ways. There is no mistaking the single most important. It is the elevation of living standards in those countries in which capitalism's complex structure successfully takes root. A calculation by the demographer Paul Bairoch makes the point vividly. He compares the changes in per capita GNP in what he called the "presently developed" and the "presently less developed" countries — that is, between the capitalist and noncapitalist worlds — calculated in dollars of constant value for three benchmark periods: the 1750s, the 1930s, and the 1980s. The "presently developed countries" enjoyed average per capita incomes that were approximately four times larger in the 1930s than they had been in the 1750s, and then again four times larger in the 1980s than they had been fifty years before. By way of contrast the "presently less-developed countries" essentially showed no increase in per capita income between the earlier two benchmarks, and then only slightly more than doubled it between the 1930s and the 1980s. Looking at the comparative performance of the two sets of countries, we see that whereas average living standards of the two worlds were much the same in the 1750s — in itself an astonishing fact — over the next 230 years the average person in the capitalist world became eight times richer than one in the non-capitalist world.[19]

One should, of course, regard these figures with some caution. One reason for the extraordinary difference in performance is the rapid movement towards population stabilization in the advanced countries, compared with its runaway growth in the underdeveloped world. Both the stabilization and the explosion of population may be indirect effects of capitalism — the first reflecting its spreading middle-class culture, the latter testifying to the powerful efficacy of its advances in public health, introduced into nations without birth control. Some portion of the divergence in income, in other words, is undoubtedly the result of side effects of capitalism rather than its superior productive performance alone. A more important reason was the drainage of wealth from the underdeveloped periphery to the developed centre — a capitalist version of a much older imperialist exploitation of the weak by the strong. The widening gulf between rich and poor nations is undoubtedly not just a measure of the superior performance of the capitalist world but also an indication of its exploitative powers.

Thus one must undoubtedly qualify the message that Bairoch's figures convey. That is not, however, to deny their striking conclusion. Capitalism has altered the course of history first and foremost by creating an entirely new socioeconomic environment in which, for the first time, material conditions have improved steadily and markedly in those areas where the system flourished. I make the point once more for emphasis. Looking back over 150 years of growth in the United States, we find that real per capita income over that period grew at an average rate of 1.5 percent a year — perhaps not very impressive-sounding until we realize that this was enough to double real living standards every forty-seven years. Moreover, with the exception of the bottom years of the depression of 1869 and the terrible early 1930s, economic activity in every year has been within ten percent of a straight line linking 1839 and 1989. More recently, we have seen this same transformative process take root in Europe, and more recently yet in Japan and along the Pacific Rim in Taiwan, Korea, Hong Kong, perhaps Singapore and Malaysia.

V

THUS THERE HAS NEVER BEEN such a social mechanism for sustained economic progress as that of capitalist accumulation. It would, however, be much too simple to depict the process, in Marx's phrase, *couleur de rose*. Unmistakable as has been the elevation of material well-being as a consequence of the successful development of capititalism, so also has been the appearance of a new form of social misery — not the ancient scourges of bad crops, invasion by marauders, or simple injustice, but an "economic" side effect that had no precursors in earlier societies. This side effect was the tendency of the growth process to generate both wealth and misery simultaneously as part of the workings of the accumulation process itself.

The new form of misery made its initial appearance in Elizabethan England as the "enclosures" of land. Enclosures meant that land traditionally available as a "commons," where poor peasants could build their huts, graze their beasts, and grow a few vegetables, was now taken over by its legal owners, mainly landed gentry, for the exclusive use of sheep grazing. The enclosures themselves were approved by Parliament and were accompanied by small payments to the peasants who were dispossessed. But they exacted a hideous price. Returning from a tour of her realm, Queen Elizabeth exclaimed that "paupers were everywhere"; 150 years later the "wandering poor," as the uprooted peasants were then being called, were still the scandal of the nation. The cause of this massive and long-lasting misery lay squarely in the introduction of capitalist processes into a still largely feudal society. Enclosures were undertaken because the sale of wool had become a profitable activity. The wool trade was without question one of the growth centres of late seventeenth century England — it is not for nothing that the Lord Chancellor of the House of Commons today sits on a woolsack. Thus considerations of "economics" both quickened the pulse of production and became a cause for disruption and impoverishment.

The "immiseration" process took a different guise a century later. By that time the active centres of accumulation had moved to the manufactories about which Smith wrote. The outputs of these burgeoning industries undoubtedly benefited the middle-class consumers who bought them, and the profits they earned certainly benefited their owners. What is not so certain is whether benefits also accrued to the workmen. Their wages were low, as they were everywhere, so that cannot be the primary problem. It is Smith himself who identified it as a deterioration in the effects of the repetitious, mindless tasks to which the division of labour led. Smith lamented: "[T]he man whose whole life is spent in performing a few operations . . . has no occasion to exercise his understanding . . . and generally becomes as stupid and ignorant as it is possible for a human creature to become."[20]

By the early nineteenth century the still small-scale manufactories were eclipsed by the "dark Satanic mills" where women and children laboured under brutal conditions for less than subsistence pay. This underside of Dickensian England is well-known, although it is not so often remarked that the same mills that appalled the more sensitive observers of the day were also centres of accumulation on a major scale, as well as one of the first sources of its overseas reach. Friedrich Engels remarked to someone that he had never seen so ill-built a city as Manchester with its hideous slums. His companion listened quietly and then said, "And yet there is a great deal of money made here; good day, sir."[21]

It was Marx, of course, who linked the two aspects of capitalism. Marx was far from blind to the material successes that capitalism had brought — the reader of the *Communist Manifesto* is always surprised to discover that it contains a veritable paean to the powers of the accumulation process. Marx's perception was essentially an expansion of

Smith's — namely, that the imperatives of accumulation imposed a logic on the organization of labour as impersonal as that of military tactics.

At this point I shall not go further into the question of immiseration — Marx's term for this dehumanization, which we can see is not the same as impoverishment. When we look to the future in our last chapter, the issue will recur, partly in the question of exploitation, partly under the heading of ecological damage. The very words *exploitation* and *ecology* are enough to indicate that we are far from finished with the damage that can be inflicted by the same drive that is the force behind the lifting of living standards. In this first approach to the problem, however, I want to introduce a second manner in which that two-edged sword reveals its capacity to cut both ways. This is to link accumulation with the recurrent tendency of the entire economy to lose its forward momentum, even to go into reverse.

Smith himself had already anticipated that the expansive thrust of a Society of Perfect Liberty would turn into decline once society built all the manufactories for which there would be a need. No doubt this was the result of Smith's generally quantitative, rather than qualitative conception of economic growth. But later economists have expressed a more dynamic version of his fear in the concern that the buildup of productive potential was bound sooner or later to outstrip demand. There have been many versions of this idea. Marx, for example, believed that accumulation would always lead a crisis of one sort or another, whether by substituting machines for labour, thereby killing the goose that laid

the golden eggs of "surplus value," or by mismatches of supply and demand, leading to crises of
"disproportion," or as a result of the ferocious
struggle among increasingly large-scale industrial
organizations.

In our own time interest has shifted away from
finding an explanation for these "cycles" of prosperity and depression towards a search for explanations
concerning the uneven pace of the long-term momentum of growth. I recall a class from my college
days in the 1930s when Alvin Hansen, Keynes's first
apostle in the United States, looked with interest at
an upward-sloping wavy line on the blackboard
depicting the succession of business cycles over time
and remarked that the bottom of one depression was
often higher than the top of a boom two or three
cycles back. Hansen had stumbled onto the idea of
fluctuations in the rate of growth, not in their "cycli-
cal" pattern, as the fundamental problem in the
instability of the system.

Many economists today have taken up that idea,
finding the principal reasons for it in two general
explanations, one technological, one political. The
first explains variations in economic vitality in terms
of the irregular appearance of technological or institutional breakthroughs that open vast horizons for
investment, such as those we mentioned previously.
The other general explanation focuses more on the
surrounding political, even cultural and ideological
milieu in which accumulation takes place, stressing
swings between supportive and constrictive political and social policies. In turn both these massive
background forces can be tied in, however loosely,

to changing configurations in the overall form of capitalism from a mercantile-based system to an industrial, and now perhaps to a postindustrial and multinational structural basis.[22]

However, instead of pursuing this line of inquiry any further, I want to close instead with a word about the nature of the capitalist order that is revealed to us when we look into the peculiar dynamics of its never-ending, never-satisfied drive for capital. It is that the instability of the system should really not be thought of as its failure, any more than its growth should be thought of as its success. It is next to impossible not to think in these terms, because growth is certainly a successful outcome of the system, so far as we are concerned, and recession is obviously a failure from the same point of view. But from a vantage point that is meant to reveal what capitalism "is" and how it works we can see that success and failure are not helpful terms. Perhaps it would be better to say that accumulation brings both success and failure — success because it is indispensable for material well-being, and failure because it is inseparable from adverse social effects, including instability. It may be that the ratio of success to failure can be changed somewhat in the direction we would like. But it must by now be clear that as long as capitalism is capitalism — that is, as long as a drive to accumulate capital constitutes its vital principle — we will not have one without the other.

III
THE POLITICS
OF CAPITALISM

I

OUR LAST CHAPTER WAS about capitalism as an economic system; this one will be about capitalism as a political order. The difference between the two is not as great as we might think — we have already seen that the life process of capital expansion has political as well as economic consequences, generating inequalities alongside material well-being. Marx, who was surely a searching diagnostician of its political as well as economic system, thought that the economics of capitalism arose from the "contradictions" generated by its drive for production, and that its politics arose from the "class struggles" stemming from its mode of distribution.

The idea of class struggle sounds stilted today, the vocabulary of another era. But Marx's perception should not be written off too quickly. Although it may lie in the background, out of sight, a tension between those who occupy the favoured positions, and those who do not, informs the politics of all stratified social orders. That is only to say that the fundamental political issue of capitalism, as of every stratified society, concerns its class relations.

We will return to this issue at the end of our

inquiry. But meanwhile, if we ask what is the immediate central political issue in capitalism, the issue that takes on an often obsessive prominence in every capitalist nation, there is no question where to look. It is the relationship between business and government, or from a somewhat more distant perspective, between the economy and the state.

We often fail to realize how remarkable this aspect of capitalist political life is, probably because we are not generally aware of one of the system's unique features: the separation of overall governance in any social order into two independent and legally divorced realms, which are at the same time mutually dependent and married for life. The closest analogue to this cleaving of the capitalist order is the division of feudalism between the authority of the church and the state, but that deep and tense relationship is dwarfed beside that which divides authority within a capitalist society.

Let me start, then, by saying a word about each side of this divide. We are all aware of the difference between "the state," with its institutions of law and order, its apparatus of force, and its ceremonial functions, and "the economy," with its factories and stores, banks and markets, want ads and unemployment offices. It is the business of the state to govern, and that of the economy to produce and distribute. We recognize that to some extent governing requires that the state lay down rules and regulations for the economy, and that the state must intervene into economic affairs on occasion; and we know, as well, that economic affairs inescapably intrude on the governing function, sometimes in ways that are antithetical to the public interest, foreign policy as an instance in point, and sometimes in ways that are inseparable from it, the formulation of economic policy as the central example.

What we do not ordinarily bear in mind is that this duality of realms, with its somewhat smudgy boundaries, has no counterpart in noncapitalist societies. In the centrally planned socialisms, for instance, there was, of course, only one realm, save for peasants' plots and a tiny "sector" of street trade. More important, there was only one realm even in such seemingly capitalistlike societies as ancient Greece, with its flourishing international trade, or Rome, which sported a kind of stock market in the Forum, or sixteenth century Florence with its moneyed life. The reason was that the governing authority of the state was legally unbounded. The idea that the material provisioning of society, gladly left to the self-motivated activities of farmers, artisans, and merchants, was not in some ultimate sense under the aegis of the state would never have occurred to Aristotle, Cicero, or Machiavelli. If the state did not much meddle in these activities, it was because it had more important things to do, such as the conduct of war and the celebration of its own majesty, and because these economic activities were sufficiently routinized, or untroubled, to be left to themselves. Thus, to sound again a theme that runs throughout this book, there was no "economy" in precapitalist societies for the same reasons that there was no "economics." To be sure, all the necessary activities of production and distribution were in evidence, but they were in no way demarcated from their larger social and political functions.

The separation begins, as we have already seen, in the political rubble of the collapsed Roman Empire, where we glimpsed the rise of the merchant class from a useful but incongruous presence in the medieval landscape to a social "estate" capable of challenging, and in the end defeating, the aristocratic world around it. This time, however, I want to stress another aspect of that epoch-marking social change. It is to call to our attention the two-sided political outcome of that economic birthing process. On the one hand, a true realm of power and authority came into existence in a network of farms, manufactories, and trading links that for the first time considered itself out from under the aegis of the state and capable of managing its own affairs with a minimum of political guidance or restraint — a kind of state within a state. On the other hand, the newly constituted economic realm was by no means ready to abandon its close relationships with — even its dependency on — the older political realm.

What we have, then, is the emergence of a social order at once divided and united. The obvious problem posed by such a division of authority was what should be the duties of each realm, and as usual, Adam Smith caught the issue precisely in his celebration of a Society of Perfect Liberty. He begins by emphasizing the newly won independence of its economic "half":

> Every man, as long as he does not violate the laws of justice, is left perfectly free to pursue his own

interest his own way, and to bring both his industry and his capital into competition with those of any man or order of men. The sovereign [we can read "the state"] is completely discharged from a duty, in the attempting to perform which he must always be exposed to innumerable delusions, and for the proper performance of which no human wisdom or knowledge could ever be sufficient — the duty of superintending the industry of private people and of directing it towards the employments most suitable to the interest of society.

In the very next sentence, however, Smith goes on to describe three duties "of great importance" that the state must still perform. They are, first, "the duty of protecting the society from violence and inva-sion"; second, "the duty of protecting, as far as possible, every member of the society from the in-justice or oppression of every other member of it", and third, "the duty of erecting and maintaining certain public works and certain public institutions, which it can never be to the interest of any individ-ual, or group of individuals, to erect and maintain because the profit would never repay the expense, though it may frequently do much more than repay it to a great society."[23]

As usual, Smith is impressive because he is so even-handed. A great deal of *The Wealth of Nations* is a polemic against the stubborn refusal of "Europe" to recognize the self-governing capabilities of a market-guided society. Smith fulminates against royal mo-nopolies and rails against the "impertinences" of meddlesome officials who seek to substitute their own wishes for those of the market. Yet his powerful desire to give private industry and capital their head does not prevent him from recognizing that government has an indispensable role to play. Moreover, by describing its duties in broad, functional terms, Smith by no means prescribes narrow limits on its role. Putting flesh and blood on the three public duties described above gives us the defence departments and ministries of capitalism, with their multifarious economic and political webs of influence; the national systems of law and order, with their courts, police forces, and jails; and the necessity to "erect and maintain" what we would call the national infrastructure, explicitly including education, which Smith esteems highly. This is certainly not a welfare state, of which we shall hear more shortly, but neither is it, by any stretch of the imagination, a kind of capitalist anarchy.

II

THE TWO REALMS OF CAPITALISM establish the framework for its political life. For the two realms are motivated by different imperatives that sometimes do and sometimes do not easily coexist. We are by now familiar with the drive for accumulation that energizes the private realm. But from earliest times the state has also had its own motivations — its *raisons d'état* — that have not only guided rulers and their entourages but have exerted a magnetic field capable of capturing individuals of all social classes. The imperative has followed many paths in different times and places, but there is a common denominator to them all — analogous to, and perhaps identical at the level of our unconscious motivations, with the impetus behind economic behaviour. That political imperative is the assertion of national identity itself, the continuance, and if possible the enlargement of national power and glory. The imperative as a whole, with its trappings and ceremonies of nationhood and its secular religion of patriotism, must look for its own explanation to the same kinds of buried fantasies that animate the insatiable thirst for wealth. How else can one explain the crowds that line the street for a glimpse of a national leader, the ecstatic surrender of self to the mystique of patriotism, or the collective madness of war?

We have only to pose the respective imperatives of the two realms to see that strong affinities exist despite their dual missions. The realm of capital cannot perform its accumulative task without the complementary support of the state, as the United States has recently come to realize after more than a decade of permitting its physical and educational infrastructure to deteriorate. As the other side of the coin, government is dependent on the healthy condition of the economy for the revenues it needs for its own goals, virtually all of which are expensive.

In this mutual dependency the realm of capital normally holds the upper hand. To be sure, the state wields the stronger weapons. The power to tax is the power to destroy, we say, but the very ability to tax would be an empty privilege if the economy were not operating satisfactorily; we also say that one cannot get blood from a stone. Thus in ordinary times the first concern of the state is to assist and support the accumulation of capital. Far from "crowding out" the private sector the government has made way for it to move in. It is not out of weakness, but from considerations of its own interest that the business of government is business, as Calvin Coolidge put it so succinctly.

By way of completing our overview of this normal congruence of interest, we should note that the relation between the realms has changed as the technological and institutional texture of capitalism has altered its dynamics. In Smith's time the role of the state was still largely identified with aristocratic views and interests and was uncertain as to its appropriate role vis-à-vis the emerging market economy. To no small degree *The Wealth of Nations* was a manual for government in his time. By mid-nineteenth century government was everywhere openly associated with the promotion of bourgeois interests at home and abroad — *Capital* becomes its exposé. In our own time the relation of polity and economy has changed again, this time with the state taking on functions needed to protect the economy from the increasingly threatening consequences to which an unregulated market could lead: unemployment insurance and Social Security benefits as instances of this redirection of the state's role.

We shall soon return to the contemporary interplay of state and economy, but one last word is necessary. When national sovereignty is threatened, capital comes quickly to its aid. This is not from quite the same considerations that motivate the government to support enterprise. The public realm will certainly languish if the needs of the private realm are not met, but the existence of the private realm is not likely to be threatened if the public realm suffers political setbacks — the capitalist order has withstood many shifts of political fortune, including the coming to power of self-styled socialist parties. Indeed, after World Wars I and II it has even survived military defeats. Thus business rushes to the support of government more from motives of patriotism and possibly also profit than in defence of principles. Perhaps one can sum it up by saying that business stands behind government in emergencies, while government stands behind business between emergencies.

III

IF THAT WERE ALL there were to the politics of capitalism, it would consist in little more than the mutual adjustment of these differing but not inconsistent goals. At its most difficult it would raise problems of the kind foreshadowed in Smith's examples — problems arising from interventions of government that interfere with the adaptability and flexibility that are the economic achievements of a Society of Perfect Liberty, and from the corresponding tendency of business to seek political advantages that may diminish the potential energy of a competitive market system.

These are by no means minor conflicts of interest — one thinks, for example, of the bitter battle in the last quarter of the nineteenth century in the United States over curbing the behaviour of big business, or more modern-day conflicts between government and business with respect to the choice between ecological considerations on the one hand and profits on the other. Nevertheless, these conflicts are no more than the everyday politics of any industrial system, not different in their origins or resolution from similar divergences of interest between planners and managers in the Soviet Union. This is not the case with two other issues, both of which spring from the process to which we turn again and again as the wellspring of capitalist vitality — the expansion of capital. As we will see, however, they involve aspects, or consequences, of that drive that we have not heretofore considered.

The first of these brings us to see capital accumulation itself from a different perspective than that to which we are accustomed. The perspective focuses on the geographic reach of the search for the resources, labour, and markets that make up the actualities of the capital-generating process. And as soon as we look with this question in mind, one realization springs to the fore. The economic reach of capital is immeasurably larger than the political reach of the national entities from which it operates. The accumulation of capital takes place on an international — perhaps more accurately, a transnational — scale that lifts it "above" the nation-states in which it locates its operating units. Overarching these nation-states, the process of converting commodities into cash, and cash back into a larger value-sum of commodities, takes place like a great stream of economic traffic moving across a bridge supported on the piers of mines, plants, offices, and research centres located in various parts of the world.

The magnitude of this transnational stream has become enormous. According to a recent study of the United Nations' Center on Transnational Corporations, the combined sales of the 350 largest transnational corporations in 1985 amounted to one-third of the combined gross national products of all industrial countries and exceeded the aggregate GNPs of all the developing countries, including China. What we have here is tantamount to a world economy within a world economy. As such, it introduces a new strain on the endemic political problem of the relationship of capitalism's two realms. From their earliest days all capitalist economies have taken advantage of differences in international costs — especially labour costs — as a primary source of capital. Keynes once estimated that the treasure brought back on Sir Francis Drake's *Golden Hind*,[24] compounded at existing rates of interest, was equal to the entire wealth of pre-World War I Britain. And until twenty years ago the largest single source of capital accumulation in the modern world was that amassed by the petroleum industry by buying oil in the underdeveloped world for a pittance.

International trade connections are not, however, the same as transnational ones. The latter do not merely involve the extraction of a commodity cheaply in one country and its sale in another, more developed one, but entail a network of production, research, and merchandising activities that are spread among many nations, some developed, some not. Thus the Chrysler Corporation, an "American" company, builds its most successful car in Canada; the "Japanese" Honda is produced in the

United States; the Pepsi-Cola company makes its products in five hundred plants located in a hundred countries; the Phillips, Asea-Brown Boveri, and Electrolux companies, all of them members of the club of 350 multinationals, are in many ways too large to be contained in their "home" economies of the Netherlands, Switzerland, and Sweden.

What emerges in this increasingly globalized pattern of production is a challenge to the traditional relationship between the economy and the state. The globalized market system stretches beyond the political authority of any single government. Faced with a network of connections that escape their powers of surveillance or regulation, national governments become increasingly unable to cope with the problems that arise from the intrusion of the global economy into their territories, most egregiously in moving jobs to low-wage countries. Worse, the degree of that intrusion is steadily growing, while the defensive capability of the state remains largely static. Thus there is emerging a fundamental imbalance between the two functions that are separated in capitalism, and from this imbalance emerges the risk of instabilities for which no remedy exists.

IV

A SECOND, NO LESS far-reaching tension also brings into question the framework of the two realms, namely, the relation between the economics of expansion and the domestic political peace of the system. We have already seen how the beginnings of the accumulation process brought disquiet to Elizabethan England through the enclosure of the commons. With growing political, although not revolutionary, intensity that disquiet persisted throughout the nineteenth century and a third of the way through the twentieth century. Save for a few placatory gestures, primary among them the introduction of the first social security legislation by Chancellor Bismarck, the response of governments to this threat was expressed in repressive legislative and regulatory measures. To a great degree this was no doubt an expression of class hostility and fear, to a lesser degree of indifference or inertia. But there is no doubt that a contributory element was the conviction that there was little that government could do to solve the problem of economic instability, except to allow the system to recover its "natural" vitality. Political intervention was not only contrary to the nature of things, but useless to boot.

The 1930s changed all that, and the second half of the century has changed it again, bringing us to the political impasse that is one of the marks of capitalism in our day. The initial change was brought on by the Great Depression that reduced gross national product in many countries by more than a third and in some by as much as half, increased unemployment to twenty-five percent of the labour force in the United States, and shrank the volume of international trade for fifty-three consecutive months. Capitalism, then, unquestionably stood nearer to overthrow or collapse than at any time in Marx's life. Indeed, in Germany, Italy, and Spain capitalism made way for a kind of bastard system that retained some of the drive for accumulation and some of the market mechanism, but that largely destroyed the partitioning of realms. The bastard system was called fascism, and the change in the relation of the realms consisted in the subordination of the economy to the state.

As we all know, the thirties were also the period in which capitalism underwent a profoundly important change in those countries where no such subordination took place. As in the case of fascism, the change involved an expansion of the role of the public realm, with a decisive difference — in the fascist states something like a seamless web of authority was once again established, whereas in the democratic nations the change took the form of a new "duty" added to those of Smith's three.

The new duty was to strive for what was called "full employment." This was very different from a subordination of the private sector to the ambitions of public sector because the expanded role of the state stopped far short of permitting it to guide, much less take over, the activities of the private sector. Full employment meant only that economic growth would be pushed to its feasible limits. John Maynard Keynes, whose *The General Theory of Employment, Interest, and Money*, published in 1936, was the Magna Carta of the change, did indeed foresee a "somewhat comprehensive socialisation" of investment as necessary to rescue capitalism from the danger of chronic unemployment, but this enlarged function of the state was rendered as apolitical as possible by Keynes's outspoken support of capitalism and his equally outspoken distaste for socialism.

The structural change he urged was therefore intended only to supplement the accumulation activities of the private sector by assuring a sufficiently high level of national spending. Keynes did not even think of using the enlarged public component of that spending to provide public investment, such as infrastructure. He wrote, tongue only halfway in cheek, that if sensible public investment outlets were hard to find, it would serve the purpose just as well if the Treasury filled old bottles with bank notes, buried them in disused coal mines, and let out contracts to dig them up.[25]

Was the Keynesian prescription the cause of the remarkable expansion that followed the end of World War II? It certainly cannot take credit for the transformative aspect to that boom. As in all extended periods of prosperity, technological advances stimulated capital investment in new areas, such as nuclear power, jet planes, computers. Of equal, perhaps even greater importance were institutional changes that stimulated demand, above all the new flow of incomes from old age retirement plans and unemployment benefits. Just as Keynesian economics could not claim any credit for the technological underpinning of the boom, so it was not, in itself, a source of its institutional transformation.

What Keynesian economics did provide was a rationale for using the public realm in a previously undreamt of way, as a fiscal agency of the capitalist order, charged as a minimal responsibility with the prevention of massive unemployment, and as a maximal one, with the attainment of full employment. As we shall see, the second responsibility was a great deal more problematic than the first. There is no doubt, however, that the first responsibility was discharged with vast success. In the United States, for example, government expenditures for all purposes had come to only about ten percent of GNP in 1929, and perhaps fifteen percent in 1935. By the 1970s the fraction was rising to a third, most of it traceable to Social Security, medicare, and similar programmes. In Europe the same transformation went even farther — by the 1970s public spending in many countries approached, and in some cases, such as Sweden, exceeded half of GNP. Thus, whether or not the postwar boom was initiated by the adoption of "Keynesian" economic policies, the welfare state that embodied their antidepression purpose unquestionably owed its existence to them.

The success of Keynesian economics did not, however, continue indefinitely. For a new challenge now emerged from the very success of the welfare state itself. The challenge was a consequence of the effect of prolonged prosperity on the bargaining power of labour. With differences from one country to the next the social position of labour changed from that of a largely nonunionized, passive group, grateful for an offer of work and unable to make militant claims with respect to its rate of remuneration, to a well-organized, generally aggressive participant in wage negotiations. As the labour market hardened, all advanced countries began to feel a powerful pressure exerted by rising wages against the level of prices. By the end of the 1970s the cost of living rose five to ten times more rapidly than in the early 1960s. After 1973, when the oil cartel added "oil shock" to the "cost-push" of the labour market, half the Western capitalisms experienced double-digit inflation.[26]

The advent of inflation, following the apparently effective conquest of depression, brought the second sea change to the politics of capitalism. On the face of it, the change was a shift towards system-stabilizing rather than system-expanding policies. High interest rates, a bane of Keynesian economics because of their depressing effect on employment, became a widely used instrument of national policy precisely because a stagnant economy, with all its problems, developed less inflationary pressure than a booming one. A climax of some kind was reached when short-term interest rates in the United States reached an unprecedented twenty percent as the result of a relentless and eventually successful campaign by the Federal Reserve to bring the United States' inflationary spiral under control. With this came the abandonment of full employment as the primary target of national economic policy. As inflation became the chief economic enemy, "acceptable" — that is, desired — levels of unemployment doubled from the two to three percent levels advocated by U.S. administrations during the 1960s to five and six percent in the 1980s. A similar shift was openly expressed in the fiscal and monetary policies of all capitalist countries.

V

WHAT HAS BEEN the ultimate impact of Keynesian economics on the politics of capitalism? The question really means: how successful has the policy of

"Keynesian" intervention been in sustaining the vitality of the system?

The answer is not simple. Despite Keynes's own measured political views, his economics was at first regarded as a radical critique of capitalism because of its explicit doubts as to the self-sustaining capabilities of the unsupported private sector. Today it is possible to see early Keynesianism in a different light, as a powerful force for enhancing economic stability and thereby moderating the political temper of the system. It is also the case that as the postwar boom continued it became ever more difficult to interest a relatively contented labour force in seeking far-reaching emendations in a social order that was working very well. Even in those nations, such as Sweden, where policies of substantial income distribution and social welfare were introduced, the aim of its "socialistic" measures was always to test the outer limits of liberal capitalism, not to cross over into the uncertain terrain of a revolutionary postcapitalist society. In the second phase of the postwar world this conservative turn became even more apparent. As successful Keynesianism gave way to chronic and endemic inflation, the anti-inflation policy of governments bore down much more painfully on labour than on capital. Thus, despite its reputation, the effect of Keynesian economics both in its early and later forms seems to have strengthened the interests of capital rather than undermining them and thereby to have served a conservative, not a radical political end.

I said, however, that I do not think the political

effect of Keynesianism is easy to assess. For if there is one conviction that is central to conservatism, it is that the system as a whole functions best when it is least constrained by government. What we find in both the heyday and the decline of Keynesianism is precisely the opposite of this. In the first period government came to be viewed as responsible for growth; in the second, as responsible for stopping inflation. In both periods the common conviction — expressed in the language of action, not in the rhetoric of politics — was that government held the key to the future, and that a failure on its part would seriously damage the prospects of that future.

This notion is not conservatism. It is the expression of an awareness that the economic order of the system is more integrally connected with, and more dependent on, the political order than used to be thought the case. In a word, what we see is the increased politicization of capitalism, for better or for worse. In the final chapter we will think about the long-run implications of this change.

VI

I HAVE LEFT for the last an aspect of the politics of capitalism that seems at first very distant from the interaction of the two realms that has been our centre of attention. It is to inquire into the ways in which the central institutions of the system connect with the idea of freedom, something that will lead us quickly to inquire what those central institutions may be. From there, no one will be surprised to hear, we will consider once again the drive for capital that energizes the system.

Is there a linkage between this drive and the enjoyment of freedom? One famous argument is that the very pursuit of wealth is, in itself, an expression of an absolutely basic freedom on which all kinds of liberty are founded. That basic freedom was first described by John Locke in his famous *Two Treatises on Civil Government*, published in 1690, as the right of individuals to own their own bodies, and by a small extension, the labour of their bodies. Adam Smith, following Locke, called this "the most sacred and inviolable" of all forms of property.[27] From this initial assertion of the right of individuals to command their own labour Locke moved to the justification of the private ownership of those things that individuals appropriated from nature by that labour; and by a seeming small, but actually very great extension, he further justified their ownership of the things that their "servants" appropriated for them. The right to command one's labour thus establishes for Locke the essential area of freedom that guards the individual against the arbitrary incursion of society. As C. B. Macpherson has shown, Locke's argument also extends that conception of freedom to cover the "possessive individualism" that becomes the linchpin of an acquisitive society.[28] Capitalism itself thus appears to be a social order that is both the embodiment and the expression of freedom itself.

It is easy to dismiss this linkage of liberty to the right to acquire wealth as mere privilege parading as morality, and it is no great feat to uncover the oppressions and unfreedoms that have been imposed in the name of the property "rights" that follow from this view of freedom. I would nonetheless propose that we consider more sympathetically the idea that there is some connection between freedom and the right to own the labour of our bodies and to some extent — the qualification is important — the wealth that this labour brings us. More precisely, my contention is that a social order in which there exists a partitioned-off economic realm is necessary for freedom, and that to date the only such society has been that of capitalism.

Here we begin with the powerful fact that no noncapitalist country has attained the levels of political, civil, religious, and intellectual freedom found in all advanced capitalisms. To make the case differently, the state of explicit political liberty that we loosely call "democracy" has so far appeared only in nations in which capitalism is the mode of economic organization.

What is important is the argument behind this connection. It is certainly not that the pursuit of capital breeds a liberty-loving frame of mind. It is rather that the presence of an economy within a polity gives an inestimable aid to freedom by permitting political dissidents to make their livings without interdiction by an all-powerful regime. Constitutional guarantees are no doubt the bedrock on which liberties of all sort stand, but the presence of a private realm within an otherwise all-embracing state is the equivalent of a neutral Switzerland in which refugees of all kinds can find safety.

It must be obvious that this refuge is far from

perfect. The economy is often loath to accommodate individuals who are considered enemies of the social order — subversive intellectuals, radical politicians, and such. The availability of private employments serves only very imperfectly to allow dissenters to preach their unpopular views with impunity. Even more egregious is the blanket apology that this justification for property offers to the abuse of economic power or the vulgarization of acquisitiveness. Not even the slightest correlation has ever been found between the degree of untrammelled acquisitiveness and the level of political liberties. Just the same, one cannot lose sight of the risk to freedom that exists in countries where no buffered territory called the Economy exists. Capitalism provides that Switzerland as part of its constitutive makeup.

IV
THE MARKET SYSTEM

I

THESE DAYS WE TEND to speak of capitalism as "the market," especially when addressing people in the those parts of the world where "capitalism" is still a suspect term. Ordinarily, it matters little what we call a thing, but in this case the choice of language makes a considerable difference. For markets are a part of capitalism, but not the whole, and the discrepancy between the two is very great. We would have had no trouble explaining to the village elders in our first chapter what markets were, because they could likely be found in every village of their country. We had a great deal of difficulty telling them what a society would be like if markets embraced every aspect of economic life down to the very choice of tasks that each individual should perform, for such a market "system" could be found nowhere in their country. And even such a market system is only a part of capitalism. As the citizens of the former Soviet Union are discovering to their consternation, a market system means the end of the long queues for bread that were a curse of life under a system of centralized command, but it also means the introduction of a queue that did not exist formerly — namely, standing in line at employment offices and looking for work.

Thus capitalism is a much larger and more complex entity than the market system we use as its equivalent, and a market system is larger and more complex than the innumerable individual encounters between buyers and sellers that constitute its atomic structure. The market system is the principal means of binding and coordinating the whole, but markets are not the source of capitalism's energies nor of its distinctive bifurcation of authority. Markets are the conduits through which the energies of the system flow, and the mechanism by which the private realm can organize its tasks without the direct intervention of the public realm. This suggests that our task in this chapter will be to separate the part from the whole, learning how this remarkable mechanism works, while bearing in mind that the real object of our investigation is the fate of the social order within which the market exerts its powerful integrative and disintegrative forces.

Nowadays one does not much hear about the Invisible Hand, Adam Smith's marvellous metaphor for the market system. The system is all too visible in the form of corporate manoeuvres or garish advertising, but "the market" has attained a degree of admiration and respect that would certainly have pleased Smith, a direct consequence, no doubt, of the economic disaster that has befallen the Soviet Union. In the old USSR almost the only goods whose supply matched the demand for them were the very special outputs of the Ministries of Defence. Ordinary goods, especially for consumers, did not fare so well. Russian consumers "shopped" by hearing rumours that shirts were available at the clothing outlet on Chekhov Street, or that the state bakery on Tolstoy Prospekt had a supply of loaves. Consumers often discovered that the shirts lacked buttons or the loaves taste. Things were more serious when certain kinds of goods, such as hospital supplies, were in such short supply that hospital deaths rose alarmingly; or when spare parts were so difficult to procure that factories were forced to make their own; or when goods for export were so technologically obsolete that they could only be shipped to subservient trading "partners." In the end the Soviet economy fell apart for lack of micro-order.[29]

In light of Soviet experience — mirrored to greater or lesser degree by all East European nations, China, and Cuba — it is not surprising that the market today enjoys a near-worshipful reputation. There is today widespread agreement, including among most socialist economists, that whatever form advanced societies may take in the twenty-first century, a market system of some kind will constitute their principal means of coordination. That is a remarkable turnabout from the situation only a generation ago, when the majority of economists believed that the future of economic coordination lay in a diminution of the scope of the market and an increase in some form of centralized planning. For reasons I will discuss presently, I believe that the pendulum will swing back towards an appreciation of planning, although never to the degree that was common not so very long ago.

All that, however, takes us into a consideration of

problems that we cannot fully appraise until we have looked into a matter that has been alluded to but not explained. It is how the market works. It is the answer to the uneasy disbelief of the village elders that a society run by self-interest could be counted on to provision its needs — a disbelief expressed more than once, I am certain, by many leaders of underdeveloped nations in their talks with officials of the International Monetary Fund and the World Bank. Until we can answer that question in our own minds we cannot proceed to the larger task at hand.

II

AN ECONOMIST WILL TELL us that markets introduce micro-order into a society. By micro-order they mean the equivalent of an Invisible Hand that leads men by the elbow to achieve social ends that were no part of their conscious intent. The economist's explanation begins, as did Smith's, from the assumption that a "maximizing" mind-set is a given of human nature. A question that immediately comes to mind is what mind-set would serve the same purpose in a society that was not a slave to acquisitiveness. For lacking such a peremptory inner directive, market systems will not work. The paradox of markets is not that they bring order out of a universe of individuals seeking only to "augment their fortunes," but that they will work only in such a universe. The problem in coordinating a society that does not cultivate an acquisitive mentality is that it lacks a force field that will exert a predictable effect on its members' behaviour. That opens the difficult question of whether some force field other than acquisitiveness might serve as well, a matter we will look into in our final pages.

Meanwhile, I see no reason to doubt that there is acquisitiveness enough to drive the market system, evidenced by the seemingly insatiable appetite with which individuals endeavour to increase their personal capital. This orientation now leads to three specific patterns of action that together produce the results that so baffled our village council. The first such pattern is that individuals will follow whatever feasible path best promotes their economic interest. This means that they will tend to seek out the best-paying jobs for which they are suited, readily leaving one employer, and on occasion even one occupation or region for another, if it pays better. The first function of a market system is thus to allocate labour to those tasks that society wants filled. Indeed, a market system cannot exist if there are barriers that prevent this self-motivated channelling of labour power, which is why one cannot have such a system in a society of slaves, serfs, or centrally allocated labour. The market is thereby linked to a Society of Perfect Liberty in more than a merely rhetorical way.

The second pattern affects the same channelling of effort with respect to the use that employers make of their capital. Also in pursuit of self-interest, they will increase the production of those goods and services for which demand is greatest and presumably profits highest and reduce production where demand and profits are relatively low. In this way, as with labour, demand acts as a kind of magnet for supply, further assuring a match between the two.

These first two effects of a market system are simple to grasp. It is the third pattern that requires some thought. This is the internecine conflict that affects the activity on each side of the market as competition develops among both suppliers and demanders. In the labour market workers vie with one another to secure the better paying jobs. In the market for products employers vie for shares of the public's purchasing power. The effect in all cases is to force prices of every kind, including wages and rates of profit, to the prevailing social level. The market system thereby becomes its own policing agency against the exactions of greed and the inequities of exploitation. Oddly enough, this self-policing process is also driven by self-interest, even when this involves reducing one's immediate gain. The supplier who will not lower a price that is out of line will be bypassed in favour of another; a buyer who will not meet the going market price will not be able to purchase what his competitor can.

I think I can sense murmurs and stirrings with regard to this idyllic portrayal of the market, and I can promise a second look that will be less uncritically admiring. But understanding must come before criticism. Let me therefore add a few more words of explication, comparing the workings of a centrally planned and a market system.

Let us suppose that there is a shortage of some good in both societies, shoes for example. In a command society shortages lead to queues, which satisfy those who are at the head of the line and disappoint those at the end. They may also lead to instructions from the consumer goods ministry to its footwear division to increase output. I say "may lead" because the process of changing schedules of output is fraught with difficulties in a bureaucratic system, where there is a powerful incentive to let things be — laissez-faire is not a slogan of planned societies, but laissez-passer may be. During the 1930s, there was a famous debate between the conservative economist Ludwig von Mises and the socialist economist Oskar Lange as to the prospects for a coherent system of central planning. Mises declared flatly that such a system was "impossible" because the planners could never amass the information that a market system continuously and effortlessly displayed in the price "signals" that told marketers what to do. Lange claimed that precisely the same information would be available in a planned system in the form of inventory levels, which would rise when supply exceeded demand and fall when demand exceeded supply. When inventories rose, planners would know that supplies had to be reduced, so they would lower prices paid to suppliers and raise them for consumers, thereby discouraging output. When inventories fell, planners would do the opposite — raising prices for suppliers, reducing them for consumers. Thus inventory levels would give the planners the exact same information that they would get from price signals in a market system.[30]

History proved Mises to be devastatingly correct as to outcome but, I think, not for the right reason.

The enemy was not an absence of information — the staffs of the planning apparatus in the Soviet Union knew when shoes were in short supply or (more rarely) in surplus. What lacked was the incentive to do something about it. Self-interest counselled leaving things alone, not doing something. Hence bureaucratic inertia was the enemy — in the end, the mortal enemy — of the planning system. Ironically, Lange had sensed that this was the crux: "*The real danger of socialism,*" he wrote in italics, "*is that of a bureaucratization of economic life.*" But he took away the sting when he added, without italics, "Unfortunately, we do not see how the same, or even greater, danger can be averted under monopolistic capitalism."[31]

What Lange should have said was something else: the great source of disorder in command economies is the absence of a framework in which self-interest leads to socially useful action. With that in mind let us now turn to the market economy, where we will suppose there is also a shortage of shoes. Here, shortages give rise to a series of stimuli that are lacking in a controlled system. Urgent telephone calls from shoe stores cause shoe manufacturers to raise production levels. In the same fashion their own increased needs will lead to urgent telephone calls to leather manufacturers to increase shipments, and this in turn to further calls from leather manufacturers to buyers at cattle auctions.

From this flurry of activity prices will rise: first at the auction, then in the price of hides and leather, finally in shoes. As production flows increase, more labour will be needed, perhaps more machinery. The word gets out that the shoe industry is hiring at good wages. Shoes come back into stock, but they are more expensive than before. Consumers buy fewer pairs per year than they used to. Expansion in the shoe industry tapers off. The shoe shortage becomes a thing of the past. A new pattern of outputs, wages, and prices has brought about a stable situation in the shoe industry: telephone calls cease. Micro-order reigns supreme, although no one has done anything but follow the arrow of self-interest every step along the way.

III

IT IS IMPORTANT to bear in mind how a market system acts in theory, because most of the time it also works more or less that way in practice — if it did not, capitalism would long ago have collapsed. I say "most of the time" because markets are working even when we are wholly unaware of them — indeed, they are working at their best at those times. As long as markets provide coherence and order, we are quite unconscious of their presence, as we would be of a planning system if it, too, worked satisfactorily most of the time. I need hardly add that markets do not always behave in this orderly and invisible fashion. On the contrary, from time to time they work in highly disorderly and attention-attracting ways, for example, when the stock market crashes or the oil market runs amok. What we need to understand now is why markets sometimes behave and sometimes do not.

Perhaps the oldest reason for market-caused problems lies in their changed characteristics in economies whose typical units of operation are no longer small, adaptable enterprises but large-scale, technologically "fixed" undertakings. The difference between the two can be described by the difference between a sandpile and a girdered structure. A pile of sand will hold its shape against many blows, but a structure of girders, although incomparably larger and stronger than the sandpile, can be toppled by the collapse of a single strategically placed beam.

Capitalist societies start as sandpiles and end up as girdered structures, which is a direct outcome of the accumulation of capital — pin factories evolving over the course of time into industrial structures as large as small towns. Smith saw the competitive process as essentially one of securing and maintaining an equality of rewards within, or among, occupations and industries. That may have been an accurate perception in the time of pin manufactories, but it was increasingly less so as the nineteenth century wore on and the contending firms became large-scale textile mills and mechanized coal mines and then truly giant enterprises, such as railways. Such enterprises required expensive capital structures, and these structures in turn imposed large fixed costs, such as interest, which had to be met to remain solvent. The result was the rise of cutthroat competition that forced many weaker firms to the wall, where they were bought up cheaply by firms that survived. Later, when cutthroat competition became too costly, the pressures of competition led instead to amalgamation by merger and trusts. In the United States, for example, most companies in 1865 were highly competitive, with no single company dominating any single field. By 1904 one or two giant firms controlled at least half the output in seventy-eight different industries.[32]

Thus the dynamics of competition itself became a major source of the transformation of an atomistic economy into one of structured strength and weakness. Alfred Chandler has shown how different national capitalisms have dealt with the ensuing threat to stability — some working out tacit agreements of live and let live, others resorting to cartels, some with and some without government agreement and approval.[33] In our own day, as we have seen, the problem has become still more complex insofar as the interconnectedness of the global economy widens the field of competition beyond national boundaries. The 350 corporations whose combined sales come to a third of the aggregate GNP of the industrial world are giant beams in the structure of world capitalism, and by that very fact, a new source of potential instability.

This possible insecurity is the same problem that we looked at in considering the changes in the balance of power between the private and public realms, and it leads to the same conclusion: there exists no effective political counterforce to undertake the fiscal, monetary, and regulatory moves that might be required to stabilize production if that transnational structure should ever begin to shake. We are in much the same condition of helplessness with regard to maintaining or repairing the flow of transnational production as we were with respect to maintaining our domestic flows of output in the 1930s.

Market disorders do not arise only from the increasingly girdered structure of production. They also have a psychological rather than a technological or organizational basis. Suppose there is a shortage in the grain markets that sends prices up. Ordinarily, higher prices would bring more grain into the market, perhaps from imports, while at the same time causing grain consumption to diminish. Micro-order will be easily restored. But now imagine that news of a potential drought reaches the floor of the grain exchange. Expectations about future grain prices soar. Thereupon, self-interest will no longer motivate suppliers to sell at what were, only that morning, very favourable prices, but to hold back for the expected higher prices to come. In the same fashion buyers will not be deterred by today's high prices, but will try to fill their needs before things get worse. The result is exactly the opposite of the textbook case: the shortage will get worse, not better.

Whenever expectations point towards a worsening of existing conditions, market outcomes will not be equilibrating but disequilibrating. An initial mismatch of supply and demand will turn into a still worse one. Thus anything that affects mass psychology adversely can reverse the effect of self-interest from order-generating to disorder-generating actions. We faced precisely such disorders during the 1930s when the bottom fell out of the grain markets as farmers rushed to sell and buyers stood around with their hands in their pockets; and something like the same process occurs during inflations when sellers are in no haste to sell and buyers can't wait to buy, thereby adding fuel to the inflationary fire.

This last phenomenon takes us out of the context of a micro-disorder into the economy-wide problems of macro-disorder, which deserves a word by itself.

For many years economists believed that markets would regulate the overall level of employment as smoothly as they did that of the level of output of individual goods. If the employment level were too low, the market would cure the problem because wages would fall as unemployed workers competed to find jobs. As wages declined, employers would find it profitable to hire more help. Thus the market would cure an imbalance between the supply and demand for labour as effectively as for a single commodity. In much the same fashion the market was also supposed to guide all saving into investment, the rate of interest serving the same function in the capital markets as the level of wages in the labour market.

But once again expectations can spoil this orderly process. When Keynes shocked the economic world of the 1930s by pointing out that the market mechanism would not necessarily drive the economy into full employment, his most telling argument was derived by applying to the determination of employment precisely the adverse effects that expectations can produce in determining the level of prices. Keynes asks us to suppose that employers see the level of wages falling and think about the effect of this on the demand for their output. Will they hire more labour in the face of such an unpromising future? Will they risk putting funds into capital projects no matter how low the cost of borrowing? The economy will still seek to balance the supply and demand for labour and for borrowed funds, but the point of equilibrium would not be the same as when expectations were buoyant.

Thus changing expectations change the outcome to which maximizing behaviour will lead, which has unexpected consequences for those who see the market mechanism as providing an unchallengeable basis for capitalist operations. Critics of the market have long pointed out that a society whose economic activities are ruled by the market will be an attentive servant of the rich, but a deaf bystander to the poor. As a result, there is always a moral vulnerability to the micro-order that the market produces. We can now also see that there is a problem with respect to the macro-order that emerges from market considerations. Here the missing element is not morality — under certain kinds of expectations the market may create more demand for employment than workers are willing to supply. There is, however, a vulnerability of an operational kind. In the case we have just mentioned the market will produce a cost-push inflation, just as under the influence of the expectations about which Keynes wrote it will produce unemployment. Neither condition will be well suited to strong and steady growth. Both will, in fact, give rise to the sorts of difficulties we spoke about last time in which the workings of the private realm generate difficulties that are likely to bring about a cry for public remedy.

IV

I HAVE KEPT for the last what is perhaps the most penetrative and perplexing of all the influences that the market system brings to bear on capitalism. It is an effect that the market imposes all the time, whether it is working silently and well, or noisily and disruptively, an effect of which we are sometimes acutely aware but more frequently quite ignorant. In its most general form it is called "market failure," but it has deeper and more insidious forms that are better described by other terms which we will come to in due course.

One of these is an undesirable market-related effect called an "externality." An example would be the higher laundry bills and health costs of people living in Pittsburgh before the pollution of the steel mills was brought under control. These costs are "external" in that, unlike the "internal" costs of the labour and raw materials that are paid by the mills, pollution costs are foisted on individuals who are external to the production process itself. Therefore steel producers have no incentive to cut down on pollution, insofar as they do not pay the laundry or health bills to which it gives rise.

As a result, the market mechanism does not accurately serve one of the purposes that it purports to fulfill — namely, presenting society with an accurate assessment of the relative costs of producing things. Suppose, for instance, that there are two ways of making steel, one of which is very clean but expensive and the other dirty but cheap. Competition will push producers to choose the cheaper way, and an unsophisticated observer will say that the market has thereby helped society increase the efficiency of its operations. It could be, however, that if the laundry bills and health costs were added into the cost, the cleaner process would also turn out to be the cheaper. To the extent that this was the case, externalities will have steered society in the wrong direction, to a less rather than more efficient choice.

I said a moment ago that these were perhaps the most penetrating and perplexing influences that the market system imposes, and a moment's reflection will reveal why this is the case. To begin, there is virtually no act of production that does not have some external effects, sometimes good, sometimes bad. An individual builds a hideous house and depresses property values along his street. A business perfects a new product and opens new horizons for its users — transformational growth is largely a matter of favourable externalities. A nation enjoys strong economic growth and thereby hastens the advent of global warming.

To take into account all the external costs and benefits of production would be impossible. At the same time we know that a failure to take into account even the more important of them seriously distorts our assessment of the costs and benefits of production. The overcutting of forests, the overfishing of the seas, the overconsumption of gasoline are all instances of externalities — that is, of a failure to include the full costs of producing various goods in their prices. Adam Smith was similarly concerned with an externality when he lamented the ignorance and stupidity that resulted from subjecting working people to mind-numbing routines, even though he did not take into account the social costs that such an externality imposed. The cost was perhaps best expressed by the late E. F. Schumacher, who observed that in "Buddhist economics" labour would not be considered an input into the production process, but an output.[34]

Externalities can, to be sure, distort nonmarket systems as well as market ones — the pollution of the East European landscape, or of the Black Sea, or for that matter the disposal of nuclear wastes in Britain or the United States can all serve as horrendous examples. What nonetheless makes externalities of special interest in a market framework is that they become another source of the border warfare between the private and public realms. Insofar as production is largely, although not entirely, carried on in the first realm, that is where externalities tend to originate, and insofar as their effects show up as costs imposed on individuals, their redress becomes a matter for action by the second. In all likelihood that border warfare will become more intense as time goes on. The volume of pollutants steadily grows; the capacity for absorbing them remains static or expands only slowly. Hence the need for government intervention rises once again to rescue the drive for accumulation from suffering its own consequences.

A second impact of the market lies in its influence on the culture of capitalism. There is more than one such influence. The ethos of "every man for himself" reflects the market mentality. The tendency to think of "production" only in terms of saleable goods distorts our view of the economy by rendering invisible public goods, such as education, public health, or infrastructure, which are not sold. There is, of course, no escaping the enthusiasms and exhortations of advertising. The sociologist Michael

Schudson has compared our exposure to smiling faces enjoying the pleasures of automobiles and laxatives to that which exposed the citizens of the Soviet Union to similar enthusiasms over coal and tractor production.[35] The difference, of course, is that Soviet propaganda was the product of a concerted and deliberate attempt to instill a kind of cultural patriotism, whereas capitalist advertising is only the product of an uncoordinated and chaotic effort to sell goods and services. Nonetheless, its effect is much the same. As the public voice of the private sector, advertising is the propaganda of a market system, just as propaganda is the advertising of a centralized one.

Schudson's assessment helps us become more aware of the wetness of the water in which we swim. I would like to heighten that awareness by comparing *commercialization*, the term often invoked to deplore the culture of advertising, with the less common *commodification*, which owes its origins to Marx. Commercialization implies an extension of the market into areas from which we feel its values ought to be excluded: for example, the devolution of the age-old celebration of physical excellence into commercial sport. Commodification refers to welcome extensions of the realm of the market into "life." We greet with enthusiasm the saving in labour time and the enhancement of personal capabilities that derive from entrusting the preparation of food, the care of our homes, the grooming of our bodies to commodities we can buy in the supermarket rather than to our private and personal skills, ingenuity, and labour. Hence, commodification is not generally seen as an intrusion into our personal domains, but as an enlargement of them, or perhaps as a democratization of refinements that were formerly enjoyed only by those who had the leisure, or could command the trained services, to enjoy what is now offered by a purchasable good.

From this perspective commodification is intertwined with the "affluence" that is the proudest boast of capitalism. I put the word into quotes because the qualities and characteristics that affluence celebrates are a highly selective sampling of the various effects that commodification brings. These effects are by no means confined to the gratifications they afford their users. Like externalities, commodification also imposes costs that, in their aggregate, may greatly diminish or even outweigh these benefits: we become "creatures" of the economy, and consumption is taken to be a measure of life itself. Marx expressed that concern by formulating the concept of "alienation" — the incapacity of individuals to grasp the nature of the social order in which they live because of their subordination to its demands. Alienation thus not only blinds us to whatever losses may result from our surrender to a commodified world, but dulls any awareness that the very vocabulary in which we appraise the performance of the economy — "efficiency," "cost," "value" — smuggles into the evaluation process the prerogatives and requirements of the social order to which that economy caters. Smith anticipated Marx when he pointed out that "efficiency" appears to be socially useful because we are blinded to its cost in the degradation of the labourer.

So the market imposes costs along with its benefits — sometimes very great, possibly even grave costs. But what could be put in its place? The question points to the conclusion towards which we have been making our way. It should be clear by now, however, that the last chapter cannot be easy to write. Never mind about the difficulties of prediction. It is conception that poses the more daunting challenge. It is no great problem to discover the deep-seated, perhaps unremovable problems of a capitalist order. It is not so easy to describe the structure of a society that will avoid these problems. I suspect that these sobering alternatives already anticipate the manner in which I shall try to describe what twenty-first century capitalism might be.

V
SCENARIOS
FOR THE FUTURE

I

I SAID AT THE OUTSET that I would not conclude with a grand prediction about the future. That does not mean, however, that I have nothing to say about the prospects for the society in which our children and grandchildren and great-grandchildren will live. It is rather that I do not think we can foresee these prospects with the clarity and scientific certitude that the word *prediction* conveys. I shall therefore speak of twenty-first century capitalism in terms of the scenarios by which we can imagine its development. *Scenario* is a term with dramatic overtones. It conveys the feeling of something more complex than a prediction — an attempt to describe processes partly driven by necessity and partly by volition, partly open to analytic understanding, partly grasped by intuition and conviction. The usefulness of scenarios therefore lies as much in their capacity to illumine the interplay of analysis and vision in thinking about the future as in the light they shed on what it will actually be.

Almost all of the great economists wrote scenarios for capitalism, but whereas most were gloomy with respect to its long-term future, their ideas about the path to that future could hardly have been more at variance. Adam Smith, as we know, envisaged a Society of Perfect Liberty whose most striking characteristic was a general increase in well-being for everyone. It is less well-known that his scenario also anticipated a time when such a society would accumulate "[the] full complement of riches" to which it was entitled by virtue of its resources and geographic placement, at which point accumulation would stop and growth with it.

In a society of small-scale enterprise such an outlook is not unrealistic, and in any event we can imagine Smith placing the fateful turning point as being as indeterminately far in the future as we generally locate the advent of a serious ecological barrier to growth. Smith's long, upwards gradient thereupon turns downwards as a growing population must divide up an output that has ceased to grow. As we have already seen, his social vision leads him to expect the moral decay of the labouring class, to which it will passively submit. Thus, contrary to his popular reputation as the tutelary figure for capitalism, Smith is, of all economists, probably the least sanguine as to its eventual outcome. Analysis points to its eventual decline; vision to its earlier decay.[36]

Marx, by way of contrast, is optimistic — not about capitalism, to be sure, but about the social order to which it will give birth. As we would imagine, the visionary aspect of his scenario is utterly different from Smith's, but as we might not anticipate, the analytic portion closely resembles it. Like Smith, Marx's analysis traces the consequences of an acquisitive drive in a competitive environment. Its conclusion differs from Smith because it replaces the pin factory with the much larger-scale textile mill so that the expansion process becomes turbulent and disruptive rather than smooth and regulative. As a consequence, Marx's upwards trajectory, quite unlike Smith's, is continually interrupted by periods of crisis and restructuring.

Yet this extremely important difference stems from their contrasting perceptions of technology, not from any deep division in social interpretation. What is ultimately more important in the full scenario is Marx's vision of the working class as the agency of its own future liberation, not the passive victim of the existing order. Smith's "stupid and ignorant" labouring class thereby gives way to a confused but slowly comprehending proletariat. Thus for Marx the scenario presents a different kind of outlook — not historic rise and fall, reminiscent of eighteenth century views of the glories that were Greece and Rome, but a directional process in which capitalism disappears before the advent of its successor, socialism.

Two other major scenarists also expect the end of capitalism, once again for different reasons and with different outcomes. John Maynard Keynes is today regarded as a scenarist of capitalist decline, but that also fails to do justice to the analytical and visionary elements in his scenario. In contrast to both Smith and Marx, Keynes was an analytical pessimist, but a visionary optimist. Analytically he was pessimistic because his understanding of the workings of the market, in which expectations played a key role, led to the disconcerting conclusion that a market-driven society could settle into a position of lasting under-employment. But very much like Smith, that pessimism reflected a static view of technological possibilities. It is doubtful if the *General Theory* would have manifested its rather discouraged tone had it been written in the postwar technological era that Keynes did not live to see.

Keynes's pessimistic analytic conclusion was, moreover, balanced by a surprisingly sanguine assessment of capitalist political possibilities. His vision included neither Smith's despairing assessment of the labouring class, nor Marx's largely buoyant assessment of its revolutionary potential. Therefore it was possible for Keynes to envisage with equanimity not only the socialization of investment "[as] the only means of securing an approximation to full employment," but also the gradual "euthanasia of the rentier,"[37] while at the same time scoffing at the idea of socialism, for which he entertained all his life a kind of benign scepticism. Keynes's vision is therefore one of a balanced polity as well as a balanced economy, a view he described as "moderately conservative."[38]

The great scenarios would not be complete without the inclusion of Joseph Schumpeter's. He is at once an analytical optimist and a visionary pessimist. "Can capitalism survive?" he asks early in his magisterial *Capitalism, Socialism, and Democracy*, published in 1942. His answer is unequivocal: "No. I do not think it can."[39] The reason, however, is not that of Smith, Marx, or Keynes. Schumpeter introduces a new and much more dynamic element into the accumulation process: Marx's ruthless destruction of old capitals by competition is replaced by a "perennial gale of creative destruction" as entrepreneurs create and exploit previously nonexisting fields for expansion. Schumpeter, therefore, scoffs at the idea that the investment frontier and its territory can ever be fully occupied. Technological possibilities, he writes, are "uncharted seas;" the airplane will be for the future what the conquest of India was for the past. Indeed, he concludes: "There are no *purely economic* reasons why capitalism should not have another successful run," at least in the short run — which, he has previously informed us in passing, is a century.[40]

Why, then, does Schumpeter nonetheless expect the demise of capitalism? The answer lies in sociology, not economics; in vision, not analysis. Schumpeter perceives the culture of capitalism as corrosive of values. The sustaining core of its beliefs, like all such foundational value systems, is ultimately beyond rational defence and it will wither under the unsentimental scrutiny of capital values. "Capitalism," he writes, "creates a rational frame of mind which, having destroyed the moral authority of so many other institutions, in the end turns against its own: the bourgeois finds to his amazement that the rationalist attitude does not stop at the credentials of kings and popes, but goes on to attack private property and the whole scheme of bourgeois values."[41] The end thus comes as the entrepreneurs who embody the élan of the system lose their enthusiasm and settle down for a secure existence as socialist managers.

Vision rather than analysis sets the stage for this

astonishing "prediction." In Schumpeter's view entrepreneurs are members of elite groups that rise to the top in all societies: socialist government will assuredly make use of their "supernormal quality." On the other hand, workers, and the middle and the lower orders generally — all creatures of habit and routine — will not even notice the difference: "a family likeness" will make socialism much more like capitalism than different from it. Will this bourgeois, managerial socialism work? "Of course it will": Schumpeter is as apodictic in declaring that socialism will work as in previously declaring that capitalism will not survive. Indeed, he goes on to say that there is every reason to believe that the morale and self-understanding of socialism may be higher than that of capitalism, and doubts about planning will come to look as nearsighted as those expressed by Smith about the future of joint-stock corporations.[42]

II

THIS IS NOT THE PLACE to enter into a detailed critique of these remarkable attempts to foresee the immanent tendencies of a capitalist order.[43] But it is a very fitting place to ask how such mutually inconsistent, often historically disconfirmed expositions can be of use in thinking about the prospect ahead.

There are, I think, two answers to the question — or better, perhaps, two lessons to be drawn from these vistas. The first is that, however diverse their analyses, their visions, and their conclusions, all of them perceive capitalism as a social order whose historical direction is, in some general sense, foreseeable. That common perception is testimony to the remarkable properties of a society energized by a universal acquisitive drive mainly constrained by the contest of each against all.

Endless textbooks have described the outcome of such a unique social configuration. All present "the economy" as a complex mixture of order and disorder, equilibrating tendencies and disequilibrating tendencies, expansive thrusts and contractive retreats. From this point of view the fact that their "predictions" disagree becomes secondary to their agreement that there exists the possibility of undertaking such a mode of inquiry to a society — perhaps I should even say the impossibility of not doing so. No other social formation displays such systemic properties — not primitive communities, kingships, empires, or the societies that have called themselve socialist. Some kind of self-determined historic trajectory is the unique hallmark of capitalism in history.

Scenarios reveal and examine these trajectories in ways that combine analysis and vision, and this interaction is important enough to warrant restatement. Scenarios come to different conclusions in part because their analytic expositions start from different observed situations or take place in differently perceived terrains. The result, as we have seen, leads to the very different outcomes of Smith's inertial sand-pile economy and Marx's vulnerable girdered structure; to Keynes's unemployment equilibrium and Schumpeter's unlimited creative destruction. Scenarios depart from one another for another reason, as well. However logical and systematic it may be, analysis must begin from a preanalytic base. The social dramas that are set into motion move along equally systemic but differing paths because the actions of the dramatis personae are differently conceived: compare Smith's "masters," many of them risen from the humble origins, with Schumpeter's entrepreneural elite, or Keynes's politically unremarkable labourers with Marx's restive proletariat.

Such preconceptions inform all social judgements. They are what endows the predictive elements of scenarios with life. They are also the reason that every scenario contains autobiographical elements, with their freight of known and unknown biases. Scenarios are therefore inescapably conservative or liberal, reactionary or radical, because they are filled with hopes and fears, as well as with objective and internally coherent workings-out of interacting elements. Thus scenarios are more than predictions in another sense. They are the answers we give to a question that, unlike a predictive query, cannot go unanswered. The question is: what of the future? There are many answers that we can accept to this query, including tragic ones, but there is one response that would be unendurable. It is silence. Scenarios fill that void. Keynes once wrote about the future that "We simply do not know," but his scenario implies that we can trust.[44]

III

THE SECOND QUESTION to be asked, or lesson to be drawn from these scenarios, is why virtually all of them perceive capitalism as self-destructive. One cannot give a simple answer where one does not exist — we have seen how diverse are the reasons behind the outcomes of our four observers. Let me, however, turn the question around: why do none of our philosophers, not even Smith or Schumpeter, who are surely partisans of the order — foresee a long untroubled future for capitalism? Why can we not find any major figure in the history of economic thought who projects such a future? Alfred Marshall, the great Victorian economist, ends his troubled and compassionate study with the hope that "economic chivalry" will carry the day and warns against "ill-considered" changes that will do more harm than good. Friedrich Hayek, who believes that capitalism is necessary to prevent mass poverty and death, nevertheless sees the nose of the socialist camel under the capitalist tent.[45] There have been, and doubtless will be, many celebrants of a capitalist order, but I do not know of any serious celebrant who has expected it to carry the day by the sheer unchallengeable power of its own performance.

I think we can give one obvious and one somewhat suppositious reason for their shared general apprehension. The obvious answer is the sheer difficulty of successfully maintaining capitalist macro- and micro-order. The more suppositious one is nagging doubts regarding its political and moral validity.

As we have seen, there is anything but agreement with regard to the first of these problems. Looking over the full history of economic thought, including a good many scenarios we have not had time to examine, we see that the crucial difficulty for maintaining economic order takes on many forms — the indeterminacy of the outlook for investment and for technology; the unequal distribution of incomes; the volatility of credit; the tendency towards monopoly; overregulation; the technological displacement of labour and the technological impetus towards cartelization; the inflationary tendencies of a successful economy and the depressive tendencies of an unsuccessful one; the vacillation between optimism and pessimism.

The list could be easily extended, but nothing would be gained thereby. The common element consists in the inherent instability of an economic system whose energies are unevenly generated and whose self-regulatory mechanism is itself volatile. In the light of its possibilities for mismatches, overshoots and undershoots, self-feeding aberrations, sheer accident and, of course, political unrest, it would take the faith of a true believer to expect hitchless growth and changeless survival. In the end capitalism's uniqueness in history lies in its continuously self-generated change, but it is this very dynamism that is the system's chief enemy.

There is no point in arguing whether this perception is correct or not — that is, whether change will or will not give rise to self-corrective adaptations. What is indisputable is the perception that runs like Ariadne's thread through the overwhelming preponderance of scenarios, with all their differences of emphasis and point of view. It is that the system will sooner or later give rise to unmanageable problems and will have to make way for a successor.

I shall come back to that central finding, but I must first put forward a more contentious explanation for this shared apprehension. It is a widespread sense of disquiet with regard to the moral basis of capitalism. Once again Adam Smith surprises us by having recognized the underlying problem. He is writing here about the determination of the wages of labour:

> [T]he common wages of labour depend everywhere upon the contract usually made between two parties, whose interests are by no means the same. The workmen desire to get as much, the master to give as little as possible . . . It is not, however, difficult to foresee which of the two parties must, upon all ordinary occasions, have the advantage in the dispute. . . . In all such disputes the masters can hold out much longer. Many workmen could not subsist a week, few could subsist a month, and scarce any a year without employment. In the long run the workman may be as necessary to his master as his master is to him, but the necessity is not so immediate.[46]

This is, needless to say, before the advent of unemployment compensation, industrial trade unions, and the welfare state, which have considerably redressed the inequality between labour and capital in the advanced industrial nations. Yet Smith has his finger on a crucial point. In a market society where employers and workers enjoyed full equality of bargaining power, there could be no systematic favouring of one side over the other. In such a society it is difficult to see why some should agree to work for others, insofar as an equality of bargaining power presumes that they would begin with equal amounts of resources. But even assuming that some would decide freely to become workers, why should their employers have left a surplus of revenues — profit — over what they paid out for wages? Why would not employers, too, be paid wages, perhaps somewhat higher than those who worked with — surely not "for" — them, or why would not profits, if there were any, be divided equally among all?

It is Marx who places this question at the very centre of his investigation into capitalism. I will not retrace his explanation of the manner in which the employer-labour bargain is resolved in a manner such that all profits go to the employer. For our purposes Marx's demonstration is interesting because it explains how this manifestly unequal relationship is made to appear entirely compatible with the idea of a system that eschews coercion. In a crucial application of the distorted perceptions imposed by commodification, Marx explains how the exploitation of labour becomes invisible in a free market, because its rules of "free contract" hide Smith's distinction between those who can wait and those who cannot.

I need hardly add that Smith did not raise the issue of exploitation, as such, although he speaks of profits as a "deduction" from wages.[47] For Smith, as for most economists after him, the larger liberties of an end to feudal relationships more than compensated for these differences in perquisites. But the issue he raises has stuck in the craw of economists. Endless pages, including not a few written by

Schumpeter, have been devoted to demonstrating that workers would not be exploited in a "perfect" market where all the factors of production were paid the full value of their respective contributions to output. The answer in all cases tells us that profits are only the name for the return paid to capital — that is, the remuneration for the contribution that capital makes to production, exactly analogous to the payment called wages made for the similar contribution of labour. That which is left unaddressed is the nature of this return to the picks and shovels that are wielded by labour. Since picks and shovels do not have bank accounts, one might expect that their paychecks would be turned over to the factors of production who made them. But, no, the earnings of capital are not paid to those who use it, or to those who made it, but to those who own it.

This poses a serious problem for those who wish to justify the moral basis of income distribution under capitalism. One might claim that the inequalities inherent in the private ownership of the means of production can be justified by the need to maintain social order. That is, in fact, the position maintained by Adam Smith: "The peace and order of society," he writes in *The Theory of Moral Sentiments*, "is of more importance than even the relief of the miserable. . . . Nature has wisely judged that the distinction of ranks, the peace and order of society, would rest more securely upon the plain and palpable difference of birth and fortune, than upon the invisible and often uncertain difference of wisdom and virtue."[48]

This explicit acquiescence before the supposed

realities of the human condition is not, however, an explanatory recourse to which many economists are willing to repair.[49] In general, then, the moral problem of ownership is avoided, as with Keynes, or explained away, as with Schumpeter. Let me therefore advance a heretical suggestion. It is that the pessimistic consensus with respect to the long-term prospects for capitalism expresses moral misgivings among those who professionally seek to justify the social order in which they live. The problematic outlook they foresee for capitalism may not arise from bad conscience alone, but I suspect that bad conscience powerfully reinforces it.

IV

IT IS TIME TO TURN to possibilities for twenty-first century capitalism. I have already said that I will not presume to write a master scenario embodying my own analytic model and preanalytic visions. I think, however, that it is possible to use the understanding of capitalism that I have tried to convey in this book — its constitutive structure, its array of widely perceived problems — to state what is feasible and what is not.

I shall begin with the problems of capitalist disorder — too many to recite, too complex in their origins to take up one at a time. Only one all-important point needs to be made with respect to these problems: they arise from the workings of the system. Some are caused by the difficulties attending the drive for capital, some by the attributes of the market mechanism itself, some by the interdependencies of its two realms. When we speak of twenty-first century capitalism, it is to these matters that we must address ourselves — not to problems of war, mass hysterias, life-threatening technological developments, population explosions in the underdeveloped world, and other apocalyptic possibilities. Perhaps these will prove to be the fatal challenges of the next century, but they are not strictly "capitalist" problems, in that one can imagine their occurrence in a world in which Soviet-type socialisms had become the dominant world order.

What can be said with respect to the problems that are unmistakably those of capitalism? There is only one answer. The problems must be addressed by the assertion of political will. In one form or another — and there are many avenues of address — the undesired dynamics of the economic sphere must be contained, redressed, or redirected by the only agency capable of asserting a counterforce to that of the economic sphere. It is the government.

A few brush strokes will suffice to enumerate the ways in which government can exercise this function. The insufficiencies of expansion that have chronically plagued the system can be offset by the addition of public demand to private demand, utilizing government as an investor as well as a consumer. The inflationary pressures that quickly surface in an uncontrolled market system can be constrained by arrangements like those found in Germany, and in different form, Japan, where labour, management, and government work out mutually advantageous controls over wage and price

levels. Taxes and subsidies can considerably allevi-
ate market outcomes that bring economic malfunc-
tion, including unacceptable distributions of
income. Taxes and subsidies can also discourage
production whose external effects are undesirable,
and subsidies can encourage those that the market
does not sufficiently promote, such as education.
Government regulations can limit the unwanted
exercise of power by labour or capital. To some
extent it can buffer or contain the exposure of the
economy to the forces of international capital. Government agencies can serve as watchdogs of the
ecological interest. Government can redress, or at
least reduce, the commodification side effects of
production.

I have but to sketch in these measures to anticipate
a storm of protestations. A few will express the
conviction that government itself is intrinsically the
enemy of capitalism, a view that Adam Smith would
certainly not endorse. Some will present the objec-
tions of economic actors whose activities we wish to
curtail. Others will voice more sobering fears. An
excess of government can lead by degrees to author-
itarian outcomes. Government interventions into
markets are often ineffective, sometimes counter-
productive. In a word government is part of the
problem, not of the solution.

It would be wrong to shrug off these protestations. Taken together they express a deep concern
with the issue of excessive government power. The
concern rises from the widely shared perception that
the reach of the public sphere within capitalism has
greatly expanded at the expense of the private. We

have already noted the tripling and quadrupling of public expenditure within gross national products. The extension of the government's regulatory powers is universally recognized. Hence, it is little wonder that any proposal to extend the reach of the public realm will be greeted with suspicion, not to say hostility.

There is, however, another way of looking at this issue. It is to suggest that the most remarkable feature of two hundred years of capitalist history has been been the extraordinary increase in the size and strength of the private sector — its rivers of output, armies of workers, masses of machinery, prodigies of technology. From this perspective we can see it is capital that has grown under capitalism, with government trailing in its wake.

From this same perspective the increase in government regulatory and welfare functions takes on a different aspect. Social Security, unemployment compensation, countercyclical fiscal and monetary policy, much regulatory intervention — in short, the main areas that have been added to the public realm — now appear not so much as independent extensions of its reach as defensive countermoves against the increasing organizational and disruptive capacity of the private realm. I should add that these extensions of government have also not diminished — indeed, I would say that all things considered, they have enlarged — social and political freedom throughout the West.

There is also a second answer to the protestations. Given the problems of government to which the protesters point, granted that these problems may be intrinsic to big government, admitted that government policies often misfire and backfire — what other means is there? If the great scenarios teach us anything, it is that the problems that threaten capitalism arise from the private sector, not the public. The saturation of demand and the degradation of the labour force that are the great difficulties of Smith's conception; the crises and contradictions of Marx's model; the inability to reach full employment that Keynes selected as the great flaw; the cultural erosion of Schumpeter's scenario — these are all failures that arise from the workings of a capitalist economy, not from any interference with these workings by the polity. What solutions, what countermeasures can there be to problems caused by the private realm except those that originate in the public realm?

If that conclusion be granted, however tentatively, a further generalization follows. It is that the success in resolving the problems of capitalism will vary with the political capabilities of different capitalisms. The fundamental properties and problems of capitalism may be the same everywhere, but its adaptive capability is not. Japanese capitalism, like Italian capitalism, is driven to amass capital, is both coordinated and destabilized by market forces, and is bifurcated into two realms; but the two capitalisms do not control, concert, or buffer the performances of their economies with equal effectiveness. Everywhere national culture puts its stamp on the deep structure of economic and political life. Here I draw on an example taken from the sociologist Seymour Martin Lipset, who compares two countries, similar in many respects, whose national characters have been shaped in strikingly different ways by a common challenge. The two countries are Canada and the United States, and the challenge was that of settling and protecting a vast wilderness. Out of this common experience two very different figures emerged as national heroes. For Canada it was the Northwest Mounted Police. For the United States it was the cowboy. One would not expect two nations that chose such contrasting representatives of admired behaviour to construct the relationship between their two realms in a similar fashion.

Thus I believe that the prospects for twenty-first century capitalisms — here I stress the plural — will depend, in the first place, on the success with which different national capitalisms can marshall and apply the forces of government to deal with those of their economies. The most likely outcome is therefore a spectrum of capitalisms, measured by the all-important indicators of social and political contentment, not necessarily by those of economic performance. This is because, in the competitive struggle for survival, economic performance becomes only a means to an end, not an end in itself. Such has always been the case with noncapitalist societies, and I believe it will increasingly become the same for capitalism itself.

If I were to hazard a description of the capitalisms most likely to succeed, I would think they would be those characterized by a high degree of political pragmatism, a low index of ideological fervour, a well-developed civil service, and a tradition of public cohesion. All successful capitalisms, I further believe, will find ways to assure labour of security of employment and income, management of the right to restructure tasks for efficiency's sake, and government of its legitimate role as a coordinator of national growth. Although no doubt the institutional arrangements to achieve this goal would vary from one nation to the next, some of these capitalisms, like the more adaptive states of seventeenth century Europe, could no doubt survive, adapt, and even flourish for a long time. And again like seventeenth century Europe, some will most likely not.

For the longer run the outcome is generally less "predictable." Two formidable self-generated problems are certain to disturb the capitalist world. One of these is the approach of ecological barriers, especially those of global warming and ozone depletion. These barriers imply a coming necessity to curtail industrial growth, with its accompaniment of rising frictions between the advanced and the laggard parts of the world as to where and how this curtailment will be effected. The second problem is the internationalizing tendency of capital that continues to outpace the defensive powers of individual governments. Thus capital itself encroaches on the political independence of nations in a manner that exposes the centre to the very forces that have sowed so much economic disarray in the periphery.

Once again some highly adaptive capitalisms may cope with these problems more effectively than others, but the matter goes more deeply than that. Insofar as the malfunctions exist on a transnational scale, they require transnational political counterforce, and nothing of the kind exists. And insofar as

the difficulties affect one or more of the basic constitutive elements of capitalism itself — its ability to go
on accumulating capital, the viability of its dual
realms of authority, and its reliance on a market
means of coordination — they put to test the historical viability of the capitalist order itself. I do not
think that any kind of analysis can be applied to the
outcome of these problems, which is to say that
visions alone will inform our scenarios.

V

I HAVE LEFT FOR THE END the question that everyone
must ask who is interested in such long-term questions. It is what could lie beyond capitalism.

Until the Soviet experience many thought that the
decisive change would be the abandonment of the
market, with all its ills and faults, for a planning
system that would guide economic activity smoothly,
intelligently, and compassionately towards the fulfill-
ment of society's needs. That expectation has collapsed,
along with the collapse of the Soviet empire. Nonetheless, I would not want to write off central planning as
a possibility for a postcapitalist order. Some kind of
"military socialism" is likely to have its appeals for
desperately impoverished nations that require
wrenching transformations for sheer survival. Planning, perhaps not of such a draconian kind, may also
have its uses for at least some industrialized systems,
if the ecological threat or the forces of world capital
require extraordinary measures of reorganization and
self-protection. One hopes that central planning of

this welcomed kind would not bring political centralization of an unwelcomed kind, a question that will likely depend to an important degree on the size of the Switzerland of the private realm that remains.

What of more benign socialisms — the much touted "market socialisms" of which so much was heard in the recent past? The prospects are not as propitious as was once thought. Markets are not easily introduced without the understructure of capitalism, as we are discovering in the aftermath of the Russian collapse. In those nations, such as Sweden, in which the idea of a socialistic capitalism was wholeheartedly pursued, the conflicts between the requirements of capitalism, above all the need to accumulate capital, and the realization of socialist goals of equality have led gradually to an impasse. Sweden remains a bright example of capitalism with a human face, in many ways a capitalism that seems well suited to survive and adapt in the near-term future. Yet its momentum has come to a halt, and it is very difficult to envisage how it can go beyond its present none-too-successful situation. Sweden — and by extension, market socialisms in general — seem to have reached a frontier beyond which it is not only difficult to go but difficult to see.

Is there a way beyond Sweden? One intriguing possibility has recently been suggested. It is a society whose mode of cooperation is neither custom and tradition, nor centralized command, nor subservience to market pressures and incentives. Its integrating principle would be *participation* — the engagement of all citizens in the mutual determination of every phase of their economic lives through discussion and voting. This principle would touch on the determination of the tasks each person performs, the goods and services produced in the enterprise in which each person works, the share that each is entitled to take from the common flow of goods. Participation thus envisages a world in which widely shared decision-making by discussion and vote displaces decision-making by self-interest alone, or by persons privileged by wealth or position to make unilateral determinations. It assumes that social and economic equality has replaced social and economic inequality as the widely endorsed norm of the society, because equality seems best suited to enable individuals to lead the most rewarding lives they can.

Could such a social order work? To ourselves, socialized into a quite different mode of life, it seems hopelessly naive, utopian, against human nature. Yet for most of the humans who have ever lived on this earth I suspect that our own lifeways would appear equally, perhaps even more, unnatural — I remind us of the consternation of the village elders to whom we tried to explain a market system. A participatory society would, of course, pose organizational problems. Its smooth functioning would require some marketlike coordination mechanism. Like any other society, it would have to generate a regular supply of labour for unpleasant or routine work. It would need to restrain individuals from pursuing antisocial ends in their economic activities. Some of these problems would be resolved by the normal pressures of social conformity. Others would require new technologies, new institutions, and above all, a new conception of how the economic aspect of life was to be integrated with social and political life. I have given only the sketchiest outline of what such a participatory economy might be like. But it is enough, I think, to indicate that a genuinely novel, technically workable, and morally compelling arrangement for the future exists.[51]

Do I therefore think it will be the direction of things during the twenty-first century? I do not. The transition is too difficult, the rearrangements too complex, and above all, the opposition too ferocious for any such truly revolutionary change to occur in so short a time, historically speaking. Participatory economics will not become the social order in the twenty-first century no matter what, catastrophes included.

Nevertheless, ideas have a life of their own. It is not impossible that at least the goals and the general social conception of such a postcapitalist order might enter our consciousness over the coming century. I should think the ideas and ideals of a participatory society would serve us to good purpose while we wrestle with the huge problems of making capitalism work as well as possible and as long as possible. During these years, when tensions and failures are more likely to be the order of the day than resolutions and successes, it will help to have another social destination in our imaginations.

Notes

1. Robert Heilbroner, "The Clouded Crystal Ball," *Papers and Proceedings*, American Economic Association, May 1974.

2. Elizabeth Marshall Thomas, *The Harmless People* (New York: Vintage, 1958).

3. Thomas 49-50.

4. See Robert Heilbroner, "The World of Work," *Behind the Veil of Economics* (New York: Norton, 1988).

5. Freely adapted from Robert Heilbroner, *The Making of Economic Society*, 9th ed. (Englewood Cliffs, NJ: Prentice-Hall, 1992) 13-14.

6. See Vernon Smith, "Hunting and Gathering Societies," *The New Palgrave*, vol. 2 (New York: Macmillan, 1987) 695-96.

7. Marshall Sahlins, *Stone Age Economics*, chapter 1 (New York: Aldine, 1972).

8. Alexander Rustow, *Freedom and Domination* (Princeton, NJ: Princeton University Press, 1980) 29, 47.

9. See Eli Sagan, *At the Dawn of Tyranny* (New York: Knopf, 1985).

10. Adam Smith, *The Wealth of Nations* (New York: Modern Library, 1937) 62.

11. Smith, *Wealth* 709-10.

12. Adam Smith, *The Theory of Moral Sentiments* (Oxford: Clarendon Press, 1976) 50-51.

13. Smith, *Wealth*, 31.

14. Karl Marx, *Capital* (New York: International Publishers, 1967) 595.

15. Smith, *Wealth* 324, 325.

16. *Capital* I: 763.

17. Smith, *Wealth* 4-5.

18. Smith, *Wealth* 700.

19. Paul Bairoch in Just Faaland, *Population and the World Economy in the 21st Century* (Oxford: Basil Blackwell, 1982) 162.

20. Smith, *Wealth* 734.

21. Edmund Wilson, *To the Finland Station* (New York: Farrar, Straus & Giroux, 1972) 142.

22. See E. J. Nell, *Transformational Growth and Effective Demand* (London: Macmillan, 1992); David Gordon, Richard Edwards, and Michael Reich, *Segmented Work, Divided Workers,* chapter 2 (New York: Cambridge University Press, 1982).

23. Smith, *Wealth,* book 4, chapter 9. I have slightly altered punctuation for ease of reading.

24. John Maynard Keynes, *A Treatise on Money*, Vol. 2 (London: Macmillan, 1953) 156-57.

25. John Maynard Keynes, *The General Theory of Employment, Interest, and Money* (New York: Harcourt Brace Jovanovich, 1936) 129.

26. John Cornwall, *The Theory of Economic Breakdown* (Cambridge, MA: Basil Blackwell, 1990) 40.

27. Smith, *Wealth,* 121-122.

28. C. B. Macpherson, *The Theory of Possessive Individualism* (New York: Oxford University Press, 1962).

29. For an excellent overview see Nicholai Shmelev and Vladimir Popov, *The Turning Point* (Garden City, NY: Doubleday, 1988) 75.

30. See Ludwig von Mises, "Economic Calculation in the Socialist Commonwealth," *Collectivist Economic Planning*, ed., Friedrich von Hayek (London: Routledge & Sons, 1935) 105; Oskar Lange and Fred Taylor, *On the Economic Theory of Socialism* (New York: McGraw-Hill, 1938) 87-89.

31. Lange and Taylor 109-10.

32. R. Heilbroner and A. Singer, *The Economic Transformation of America: 1600 to the Present*, 2nd ed. (New York: Harcourt Brace Jovanovich, 1984) 202-03.

33. Alfred Chandler, *Scale and Scope: The Dynamics of Industrial Capitalism* (Cambridge, MA: Harvard University Press, 1990).

34. Ernst F. Schumacher, "Buddhist Economics," *Small Is Beautiful* (New York: Harper & Row, 1975).

35. Michael Schudson, *Advertising: The Uneasy Persuasion*, chapter 4 (New York: Basic Books, 1984).

36. Smith, *Wealth*, 94. See also Robert Heilbroner, "Paradox of Progress: Decline and Decay, *Essays on Adam Smith*, ed. A. S. Skinner and T. Wilson (Oxford: Clarendon Press, 1975).

37. Keynes, *General Theory*, 376, 378.

The CBC Massey Lectures Series

Available in fine bookstores and at www.anansi.ca

38. Keynes, *General Theory* 377.

39. Joseph A. Schumpeter, *Capitalism, Socialism, and Democracy* (New York: Harper & Row) 163.

40. Schumpeter 84, 87, 118, 163, and 163, note 7.

41. Schumpeter 143.

42. Schumpeter 196, 198, 203, 204, and 211.

43. For a detailed analysis see Robert Heilbroner, "Analysis and Vision in the History of Modern Economic Thought," *Journal of Economic Literature*, September 1990, 1097-1114.

44. J. M. Keynes, "The General Theory of Capital," *Quarterly Journal of Economics*, February 1937, 209f.

45. Alfred Marshall, *Principles of Economics* (London: Macmillan, 1936) 732; Friedrich Hayek, *The Fatal Conceit* (Chicago: University of Chicago Press, 1988) 27.

46. Smith, *Wealth*, book 1, chapter 8. I have considerably condensed the original.

47. Smith, *Wealth*, book 1, chapter 4.

48. Keynes, *Moral Sentiments*, part 4, section 2, chapter 1.

49. An exception is John Stuart Mill, who writes: "While minds are coarse, they require coarse stimuli, and let them have them." *The Collected Works of John Stuart Mill*, vol. 2 (Toronto: University of Toronto Press, 1981) 209.

50. Seymour Martin Lipset, *The First New Nation: The United States in Historical and Comparative Perspective* (New York: Basic Books, 1963) 251.

51. My description is drawn from Michael Albert and Robin Hahnel, *Looking Forward: Participatory Economics for the Twenty-first Century* (Boston: South End Press, 1991). There is a companion volume aimed at the sceptical economist: *The Political Economy of Participatory Economics* (Princeton, NJ: Princeton University Press, 1991).